JOHN DUNN'S

ANSWERS
PLEASE

John Dunn is one of radio's longest-serving and tallest presenters, and he has a clutch of awards to prove it – three from the TV and Radio Industries Club, a Variety Club Silver Heart and the *Daily Mail* Silver Microphone. Since 1973 he has hosted his own BBC Radio 2 early evening show which reaches over five million listeners each week.

JOHN DUNN'S

ANSWERS PLEASE

JOHN DUNN & COLIN MARTIN

BBC BOOKS

Published by BBC Books
a division of BBC Enterprises Ltd
80 Wood Lane, London W12 0TT

First published 1994

ISBN 0563 37063 7

Designed by Gwyn Lewis

Set in Gill Sans and Bembo by Phoenix Photosetting, Chatham, Kent
Printed and bound in Great Britain by Clays Ltd, St Ives plc
Cover printed by Clays Ltd, St Ives plc

Contents

Introduction

Although no one has ever asked us about **aardvarks**, or why strip-cartoon characters go **Z-z-z-z-z-z-z-z-z** when taking a nap, we've had pretty well everything in between! *Answers Please* began on my Radio 2 evening programme ten years ago almost by chance in response to a number of unsolicited questions from listeners. We decided to make them into a programme, asked if there were any more out there and we were away.

As you will see from the selection, the great thing about Tuesday evenings is the variety of topics you bring up: questions you'd always wanted to ask, questions you'd never thought of asking, questions that were easy to answer and a fair number that completely stumped us. And I do mean 'us' – I would like to take this opportunity to thank the small army of researchers who have worked on *Answers Please* over the ten years. If it has been a chore, they have never shown it even though I know that an apparently simple query can take half a day and a dozen phone calls to answer. And as most of your questions were researched on the phone, our thanks also to the many experts who have been so generous with their time – I only hope they feel their answers were accurately delivered.

But the main credit for the success of *Answers Please* belongs to our questioners. The names that appear at the end of the book are but the tip of a loyal and inquisitive iceberg. Thank you!

John Dunn

When did advertising start?

Who has vehicle licence number **AI** and when was it issued?

It was issued in 1903 and came into effect on 1 January 1904. The recipient was Earl Russell, later Under Secretary for Air, who queued all night to get it. It was subsequently owned by the rubber company John Bull who were taken over by Dunlop who, in turn, have been taken over by BTR Plc. It was last seen on a Range Rover but who was the driver? According to the DVLC: 'That is not the sort of information we are allowed to divulge.'

When was '**Abide With Me**' first sung at a Cup Final?

It was first chosen in 1927 because it was said to be Queen Mary's favourite hymn and soon became a regular part of match preliminaries. An attempt was made to drop it in 1959 when it was replaced by the Coventry Ladies Keep Fit Team. The resulting outcry included letters to *The Times* forcing organisers to reinstate it. It has been sung ever since.

When did **advertising** start?

Advertisements were found on the walls of ancient Pompeii, but advertising started in England with the birth of printing. William Caxton set up his press at Westminster in 1476 and printed a long and varied list including Chaucer's *Canterbury Tales*. But he advertised his own wares when he announced the completion of *The Pyes of Salisbury*, a book containing rules for the guidance of priests in the celebration of Easter. The first newspaper advert is thought to have appeared in 1642 during the Civil War and in 1657 a weekly paper solely concerned with advertising was launched in London.

What does the legal term aggravated mean, as applied to burglary or rape?

The Law Society gave us the following definition: 'An aggravated burglary is a crime in which the agent uses any article made or adapted for use for causing injury to, or incapacitating, a person, or intended by the person having it with him for such use.' So if a burglar carries a cosh or a knife, he has aggravated the crime. This also includes imitation weapons. If a crime is carried out with an imitation firearm, the law makes no distinction whether or not the weapon was capable of being fired.

How much did America pay for Alaska?

Alaska was bought by America from Russia for $7 200 000, which works out at less than two cents an acre. Even so it was known as 'Seward's folly' or 'Seward's icebox' after the American Secretary of State who negotiated the deal.

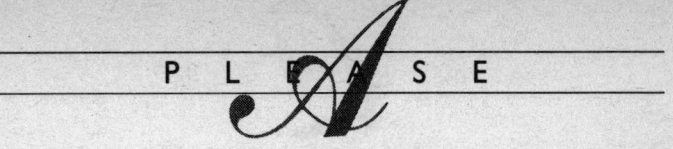

Why do several football clubs have **Albion** in their title?

A story is told that Stirling Albion was formed in 1945 by, among others, a local coal merchant who lent two of his lorries to be used as a grandstand for the opening match. They were Albion lorries! Alas it seems it is only a story because the word was around in football in the nineteenth century. West Bromwich Albion used to be called the West Bromwich Strollers until 1881 when their name was changed 'after another part of the town', the brochure says. (Which could also be the part which gave the lorry its name.)

Albion is the poetic name for Britain or England in the same way that Cambria was Wales and Hibernia, Ireland. Perhaps the clubs were simply being patriotic.

Is **alcohol** more intoxicating when drunk at altitude than on the ground?

The atmospheric pressure even in a pressurized aircraft is lower than it is on the ground, so the alcohol enters the bloodstream faster. In other words the higher you go, the higher you get! But there are other reasons why doctors advise against drinking alcohol on flights. Alcohol affects the body's ability to use oxygen efficiently and since there is less oxygen in an aircraft cabin you need all you can get. It also has a dehydrating effect on the body and since the humidity in a cabin is about 2% compared to the 30% we are used to, not only do you get drunk quicker, the hangover is worse.

What does Amen mean?

It is the Hebrew word for 'so be it,' or 'surely'. The Hebrew root word from which it is drawn is '*aman*' meaning 'be faithful; be trustworthy'.

What is the story of the Angels of Mons?

The Battle of Mons took place on 23 August 1914, within three weeks of the start of the First World War. It ended with the British army in retreat and the Germans occupying the town. At one point, it is said, angels appeared in the sky above the battle line. The British counter-attacked and for a short while the Germans were on the defensive.

The origins of the story are difficult to trace but it caught the public imagination and by October 1915 several accounts had been published, including *Back of the Front* by Phyllis Campbell who claimed that as a young nurse she had heard of the sightings from wounded soldiers. Probably the best candidate for the source of the legend however is a story called *The Bowmen* in which British soldiers are helped by ghostly bowmen in their fight against the Germans. Written by Arthur Machen just after the Battle of Mons, it was published by the *London Evening News* and reprinted in a collection of his stories a year later.

Who were the Four Horsemen of the **Apocalypse**?

They were part of the prophetic vision of St John as recorded in the Book of Revelation in the New Testament. The colours of the horses are white, red, black and pale. The first two represent warfare and the last two famine, pestilence and death. They deal with the 'great day of wrath' toward the earth. This very powerful image has often been used by artists, notably the Spanish writer Vincenti Balsco Ibanez, whose book about the First World War was called *The Four Horsemen of the Apocalypse*. It was filmed in 1921 and remade in 1961.

Why does one rotten **apple** spoil the barrel?

Apples like many other fruits, particularly red fruits, give off the gas ethanol when ripe. This has the effect of accelerating the ripening process in other fruits. One ripe tomato placed among green ones will help turn them red. Try it!

Why is **April Fools' Day** so called and why do the French call it *Poisson d'Avril*, 'April Fish Day'?

Before the introduction of the Gregorian calendar in the sixteenth century, 25 March was the start of the new year. It was also the start of an eight-day festival culminating on 1 April which was 'a day of extraordinary mirth and activity', a day when fools came into their own.

Poisson d'Avril is a French pun. They too had new year

celebrations ending on 1 April and *poisson* is a corruption of *poison* or mischief. Today in France you are liable to have a cardboard fish hung on your back on 1 April.

What had **Archimedes** discovered when he leapt from his bath shouting 'Eureka'?

Archimedes, the Greek mathematician, had been asked to discover whether or not the king of Syracuse's crown had been made of gold alloyed with silver. When he stepped into the bath and the water overflowed, he realized that displacement of water could provide him with the answer. A given volume of pure gold would not weigh the same as a mixture of gold and silver, so he measured the water displaced by the crown and then measured the water displaced by an equal weight of pure gold. History does not relate if the king had been cheated by his crown makers!

What was Walter **Arnold**'s place in history?

Walter Arnold of East Peckham was the first motorist to be convicted of speeding in Britain. In 1896 he drove at 8 mph in a 2 mph limit past the house of a policeman who chased him for five miles on a bicycle. He was fined one shilling (5 new pence), plus costs.

Who was the Maid of **Astolat**?

Otherwise known as the Lady of Shalott, she was the young lady in Arthurian legend who died from unrequited love for Sir Lancelot and who lives on in the Tennyson poem.

She was also a railway engine. In the 1920s, Southern Railway introduced the King Arthur class N.15 locos, one of which was the Maid of Astolat. They were replaced by BR in the 1950s.

What does **Aston** mean?

As in Steeple Aston, North Aston, Middle Aston, Little Aston and Aston Villa. It derives from the Old English word meaning 'east'. It later came to acquire the more general meaning of 'enclosure', 'homestead', or 'village'. It also has another, less common, meaning of 'where the ash tree grows'. So perhaps soccer team Aston Villa once played football in the garden of the villa among the ash trees!

Where was the lost island of **Atlantis**?

We have Plato to thank for the legend of Atlantis – the island continent said to have existed beyond the Straits of Gibraltar and which probably gave its name to the Atlantic Ocean. The story of its destruction by an earthquake was said to have been told to the Greeks by Egyptian priests. As with so many legends, the grain of truth it contains could have been provided by the volcanic eruption that destroyed

Santorini around 1500 BC. All that remains now are the islands of Thera and Therasis. That cataclysmic event has also been blamed for the collapse of the Minoan civilization and in 1966 a well preserved Minoan tower was discovered on Thera.

Who invented the **ballpoint** pen?

The ballpoint was invented by the man who gave it its name, Lazlo Biro. Hungarian by birth, he fled to Argentina with his brother George in the 1930s but the Second World War found him in Reading. With backing from British financier Henry Martin he designed a 'writing-stick' for use at altitude by pilots in the RAF.

When was the title **Baronet** introduced?

King James I introduced the title of Baronet in 1611 as a way of raising money to finance sending troops to quell a rebellion in Ulster. Initially 200 were offered for sale to gentry with estates that brought in at least £1000 a year. The recipient had also to guarantee the pay of 30 soldiers at 8 pence a year for three years. In time, yet more money was needed to fund the military presence in Ulster so the conditions were dropped and anybody with enough money could buy himself a Baronetcy.

The earliest title went to Nicholas Bacon of Redgrave in Suffolk who became 'The Premier Baronet' in 1611. The title was purely honorary, so no Baronet can sit in the House of Lords, but it is hereditary, being passed down the male line of the family. There have been occasional exceptions to this in Scotland. One woman, Dame Mary Bowles, was created a Baronet in 1635 – no one knows why – and the title passed to her grandson. But when he died, so did the title.

Why was the precursor to the **BBC** known as 2-LO and not 1-LO?

It was thought that on paper the number 1 would be confused with the letter I. So there never was a 1-LO. The LO refers to London.

Who are singing along with the **Beatles** on the final chorus of 'Yellow Submarine'?

Ringo sings the lead and John and Paul are the two talking in the middle. The submarine effects are created by John blowing bubbles through a straw and George swirling water in a bucket. On the final chorus they are joined by Mal Evans (road manager), Neil Aspinall (the Beatles' personal assistant), George Martin (producer), Alf ??, Geoffrey Emerick (engineer) and Patti Harrison (née Boyd – George's wife).

Who was **Beau Brummell**?

George Bryan Brummell was born in 1778 and became a close friend of the Prince Regent, later George IV. His rise to fame began when he left the army and made a career out of being a dandy. He introduced the novel idea of washing and spent two hours a day soaping and scrubbing with a stiff brush before getting dressed. Once clothed, he was reluctant to allow himself to be exposed to even the slightest breeze for fear it would ruffle his hair so he ordered his sedan chair to collect him from inside the house. He would never lift his hat to a lady because he worried he would be unable to replace it at the right angle, nor would he turn his head to speak to a neighbour in case he creased his cravat.

He went too far when he met an extremely overweight Prince walking with Lord Alvenley in Bond Street one day. 'Ah Alvenley,' said Beau Brummell, 'Who's your fat friend?' The Prince burst into tears and never spoke to him again. In 1810, Beau Brummell fled to France to escape his creditors where he died in an asylum in 1840.

How does a **bee-eater** avoid being stung internally?

Not all bees sting and the bee-eater has extremely good eyesight which enables it to tell from about 15 metres away whether or not a particular bee is a stinger. If it is, once caught the bird bashes it to death and then smears the bee's corpse along a branch to remove the sting. An internal sting – even for a bee-eater – would not be a good idea!

What is 'bee wine' and what is the 'bee' that rises
and falls in the bottle during fermentation?

What is '**bee wine**' and what is the 'bee' that rises and falls in the bottle during fermentation?

Bee wine is another name for ginger beer. The 'bee' is the yeast mass that causes fermentation in the bottle. When lying at the bottom it gives off carbon dioxide, causing it to rise to the surface where it discharges the gas and sinks again.

Is it true that the **Belisha beacon** is named after Major Belisha?

Yes. Belisha beacons are named after Leslie Hore-Belisha, the Minister of Transport in 1934 when they were first introduced. He had been a major in the Royal Army Service Corps during the First World War. The appearance of his beacons at the new road crossings aroused a great deal of public interest. There was even a rhyme that some may remember:

> A little dog walked down the road
> And not a tree in sight
> But thanks to Hore-Belisha, now
> That little dog's all right!

What is a **berry bug**?

A berry bug is a type of tick that looks like a small black-berry pip – hence its name. It is a relative of the spider family, possessing eight legs, and lives in long grass waiting for a passing sheep or human with bare legs. It fastens itself on then feeds on blood until it is full when it drops off to await the next victim. Common in the Highlands of Scotland, it is a very good reason for wearing trousers rather than a kilt!

What is or was a **bezant**?

Is and was – there are still a number around. The bezant was the coin of the Byzantine Empire and is more commonly known in collecting circles as a solidus. It contained 2.5g of gold and ceased to be produced in the middle of the fourteenth century.

How many words are there in the **Bible**?

The Bible is made up of 66 books and was written over a period of 1600 years by some 40 different writers. It is the world's bestselling book, according to the *Guinness Book of Records*, with 2 500 000 000 copies printed between 1815–1975. It is available to around 98% of the world's population.

According to one count there are a total 31 181 verses, 724 692 words and 3 671 480 letters. The word 'and' occurs 35 543 times in the Old Testament and the word 'Reverend' once. 'Lord', or its equivalent 'Jehovah', occurs 7698 times.

Who did the counting? The Prince of Granada, so the story goes, was imprisoned in Madrid for 33 years with nothing to read but the Bible.

Britain may not have a written constitution but has a **Bill of Rights**. What are those rights and where can one obtain a copy of the document?

After the Glorious Revolution of 1688, when the pro-Catholic James II was overthrown, William and Mary came to the throne having agreed to a Bill of Rights which established a constitutional monarchy in England. It stated that the monarch must rule according to the law and with the consent of Parliament. MPs were to be freely elected, were guaranteed freedom of speech within Parliament and it excluded Roman Catholics from coming to the throne.

To read the full text, ask at your local library for volume eight of *English Historical Documents, 1600–1714.*

How did **Bing Crosby** get his name?

Christened Harry Lillis Crosby, he became 'Bing' at the age of seven when the family were living in Spokane, Washington State. Here, the young 'Bing' befriended Valentine Hobbart, the boy next door. Both were fans of a Sunday comic strip character called Bingo who possessed large protruding ears. Because Crosby's ears stuck out, Valentine dubbed him Bingo which soon became Bing. Years later, Hollywood had Crosby's ears pinned back.

Do birds have a sense of smell?

Some species have a very well-developed sense of smell. The South American vulture uses it to track down carrion and the kiwi, a nocturnal bird, sniffs out worms and other tasty morsels in the dark. Birds also have a sense of taste although they could hardly be called gourmets. The average chicken has 340 taste buds compared to the average human's 9000.

Why should you not eat blackberries after 10 October?

Because superstition says the Devil spits on them on that day.

Before the change from the Julian to the Gregorian calendar, 10 October was chosen as the feast of St Michael, the day on which it was said he threw the Devil out of Heaven whence he landed in a blackberry bush. (The 'Feast of St Michael and All Angels' now falls on 29 September.)

Where does the word Blighty, used by troops serving abroad to mean Britain, come from?

It comes from the Hindustani word *bilayati* meaning 'a foreign land' or, by implication, Britain. The soldiers serving in India picked it up and it went with them to the trenches of the First World War.

Why is the sky **blue**?

Light is made up of all the colours of the rainbow – literally. When light from the sun meets the earth's atmosphere, it is scattered by the molecules of the air. Its blue component is scattered more easily than the longer-wavelength red component. The reason that the sun looks yellow is that white light with the blue removed is yellow.

When did the **blue lamp** become the symbol of the police force?

In the early nineteenth century, Westminster City Council decreed that all police stations were to have a distinguishing light outside their door. Originally it was candlelit and plain white but, with the advent of street lighting, this was changed to blue. However it was only after the 1949 film *The Blue Lamp* which starred Jack Warner as P.C. George Dixon (who later came to television as *Dixon of Dock Green*) that it became recognized as a symbol of the police force.

We discovered two London police stations that do not have a blue lamp: Bow Street, where Queen Victoria was aesthetically unamused by the blue glow when visiting the Opera House, and Northwood, where the council and local residents objected to the light on the grounds that it was advertising!

What does 'Once in a **Blue Moon**' mean?

The expression goes back at least as far as 1528 when it came to mean 'never'. However, on rare occasions, the moon may actually appear blue because of dust storms and cloud banks or ice crystals in the atmosphere. After the eruption of the volcano Krakatoa on 27 August 1883 there was a blue moon and one was seen on 26 September 1950 after huge forest fires in Canada.

Blue is not the only reported unusual colour for the moon. On 17 January 1884, a green moon was sighted over Stockholm for three minutes and again on 14 February at Kalmar in Sweden.

'Bobby Shaftoe's gone to sea, Silver buckles on his knee.' Yes – but who was he?

The answer usually given is that he was Robert Shaftoe, who stood as Member of Parliament for Whitworth in 1761, and was popularly known as Bonny Bobby Shaftoe. His supporters even wrote him a special verse:

> Bobby Shaftoe's looking out,
> All his ribbons flew about,
> All the ladies gave a shout,
> Hey! For Bobby Shaftoe.

However, further investigation suggests that the song had been around for a while before that and it may have been sung about one of the Shaftoes of Benwell. There was also a Shaftoe of Bavington who was said to have run away to sea to escape the attentions of a lady. But when all the arguing has stopped and you return to the original tune, you find it is dated 1694 and called 'Brave Wully Forster'! I think we'll stop there.

Are **brown eggs** more nutritional than white eggs?

They may look healthier, like a person with a sun tan, but brown eggs are no better or worse for you than white eggs. However 95% of eggs in Britain these days are brown.

Egg colour depends on the breed of the laying hen. The four main brown-egg hens are the Ross Brown, the Isa Brown, the Hisex Brown and the Shaver Brown.

Why is a dollar called a **buck**?

It appears to have derived from the time when skins were classified as 'bucks' and 'does', the buck being the more valuable. The US government used to pay trappers at the rate of a dollar apiece for a 'buckskin'.

Where does the word **budget** come from?

From the old French word for a bag or pouch – *bougette*.

When the Chancellor of the Exchequer presents his budget to the Commons it is an occasion full of tradition. The 'bag' itself, held up for the camera as he leaves 11 Downing Street, is said to have been made for Gladstone around 1860 and is known as the Gladstone Box.

The longest Budget speech ever, made by Gladstone in 1853, lasted 4 hours 45 minutes. The shortest was delivered by Benjamin Disraeli in 1867 and lasted only 45 minutes.

Another tradition is that the budget speech is the only occasion when alcohol is permitted in the Chamber – this is to allow the Chancellor to refresh himself. Gladstone is said to have preferred a cocktail of eggs, sherry and ether while Disraeli favoured brandy and opium pills. But spare a thought for Lord Brougham who is said to have refreshed himself so frequently that while entreating his fellow peers in the House of Lords to accept the budget proposals, he slid helplessly to his knees and was unable to get up again.

'History is bunk', said Henry Ford. What an odd word! Where does it come from?

It is 100% American. In North Carolina there is a county called Buncombe which returned a member to Congress who distinguished himself by talking rubbish and at length, much to the annoyance of the other Congressmen. His only defence when taken to task over it was that he was 'not speaking to the House but for Buncombe'. Buncombe became bunkum which became bunk.

For the record, Henry Ford did not quite say 'history is bunk'. What he actually said, in an interview in the *Chicago Tribune* on 25 May 1916, was: 'History is more or less bunk. It's tradition.'

Is it possible to be **buried** at sea?

Yes. First a licence has to be obtained from the Ministry of Agriculture and Fisheries. This costs nothing, but there are certain regulations that have to be complied with, such as how the body is prepared and when the burial can take place. Fishermen are reluctant to charge for taking their boats out for a burial, but they would ask for a donation to be sent to the Royal National Lifeboat Institution or other similar organization. The cost of a burial at sea would depend on the Funeral Director (a solid coffin is still required), but we were told it usually falls somewhere between the cost of cremation and burial on land.

Why do men **button** left-over-right and women right-over-left?

There is no simple answer to this question. Men, it is generally agreed, traditionally button left-over-right to make the drawing of a sword worn on the left easier. If the coat buttoned the other way the hilt could easily get caught. The mystery is why women's clothes should button the other way! Up to the end of the nineteenth century both men and women buttoned the same way. One suggestion is that it is easier for nursing mothers to undo their buttons with the left hand to feed a baby – assuming babies are held on the right arm! During the Second World War, men's and women's uniforms buttoned the same way for ease of manufacture.

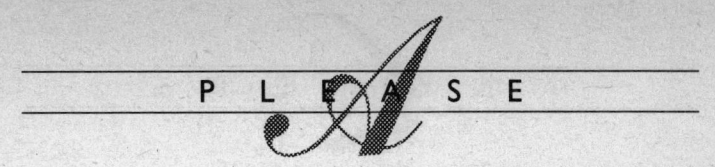

Is it possible to be buried at sea?

Why is a **Caesarean** birth so called?

Julius Caesar is said to have been delivered that way – which is how he got his name (the Latin word *caedere* means to cut). There is little evidence to suggest it was an unusual operation in Roman times but if a woman was dead or dying with a child still in her womb, then it would be 'rescued' by what we now call Caesarean Section.

Who was **Calamity Jane** and how did she earn her name?

Martha Jane Cannary, born probably in Princetown, Missouri, around 1848, swore like a trooper, drank hard, chewed tobacco and was an excellent shot. She claimed to have joined the army and ridden against the Sioux Indians but was discharged when it was discovered she was a woman. 'There's Calamity,' they cried as she roamed from bar to bar and the nickname stuck.

The stories told of Calamity Jane around Deadwood are many and sometimes dubious. Perhaps the best was that when she was watching a performance of *East Lynne* at the Opera House, exasperated by the behaviour of the heroine she stood up and let fly at the stage a stream of tobacco juice scoring a direct hit. With the house in uproar, she tossed a gold piece on to the stage saying: 'That's for your damned dress,' and walked out.

Is the calorie value of food the same whether it is hot or cold?

The calorie is a unit of heat: the amount of energy required to raise the temperature of one gram of water by 1°C. The 'calorie value' of food is hence a potential energy, released when that food is digested. It is this energy which (amongst other things!) maintains the body's temperature at around 37°C. Food taken into the body has the same potential energy value whether it is hot or cold, so there is no need to worry about a warm drink being more calorific than a chilled one!

Is it possible to turn a yellow canary orange by adding something to its feed?

Strangely it is. A substance called carophyll, which contains an extract from the cochineal beetle, acts like a dye. If added to the food it is absorbed into the canary's body and colours the feathers. We were assured it does the bird no harm and only lasts until the next moult when the feathers drop out. Flamingoes, which are pink in the wild, lose their colour in captivity and are often fed carophyll to keep them pink.

Is there any way to stop a candle dripping?

Try soaking the candle overnight in salted water or sprinkle a little salt around the base of the wick before lighting. Alternatively, rub the candle with damp soap. Another suggestion is to hold the candle by the wick, paint it with clear varnish then leave to harden. This will also make it burn longer, as will putting your candle in a freezer for a few hours before use.

The carat is used to measure diamonds and gold. What is a carat?

It was discovered that when the seeds of the carob tree were dried they were all almost always exactly the same weight. So, they were used as a method of weighing precious stones, especially diamonds. Four carob seeds become one *qirat* or carat – now standardized as 0.2g.

In gold the carat is used as a measurement of purity. It is an expression of the number of parts of gold in an alloy, the maximum being 24. So 'pure' gold is 24-carat while 9-carat gold contains only 9 parts of gold per 24.

What are the Cargo cults of New Guinea and Melanesia?

It was believed by tribes of those regions that through ritual and supernatural power they could acquire the consumer goods they assumed gave Western countries their power. So, for example, they attempted to lure passing aircraft out of the skies by making dummy landing sites on the ground. In the Republic of Vanuatu (formerly the New Hebrides) it was thought that a Second World War soldier, Sergeant John Frum of the US Medical Corps, was in some way 'King of America' and that he would send them Liberator bombers

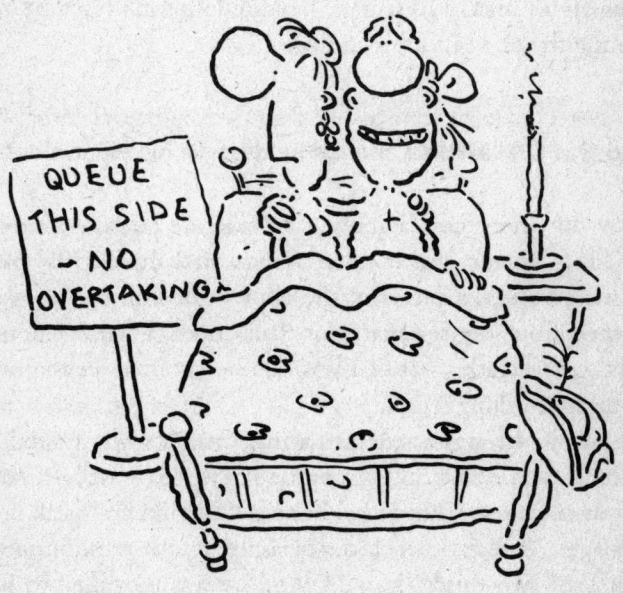

Who was Casanova and did he deserve his reputation?

with cargoes of milk and ice-cream. $75 000 was raised by cult members on the Bismarck Archipelago to 'buy' Lyndon Johnson. They intended to make him King of New Hanover in return for his Cargo secrets. Lyndon Johnson's reaction on learning the news is not recorded.

Who was **Casanova** and did he deserve his reputation?

Giovanni Giacomo Casanova, Chevalier de Seingalt to give him his full name, was born in Venice on 2 April 1725. His mother favoured a career in the church for him but he was expelled from the seminary for 'bad conduct' (and I don't think we need ask what that was). So he became free to pursue his true calling!

In his life he was a violinist, a magician, a spy, a writer, a diplomat and above all, a libertine. He once refused the famous courtesan Kitty Fisher because he could not speak her language. 'Without speech the pleasure of love is diminished by at least two-thirds,' he said. And he was mortified to be turned down by the only woman he loved, La Chaprillon, who preferred instead a barber's apprentice. 'On that fatal day I began to die and ceased to live.' Otherwise, according to his memoirs, his life was spent in the pursuit of the fair sex. For two years he was imprisoned in the Doge's Palace, Venice, where his name can be seen carved on the wall. The fingerprints of thousands of tourists wore it out but it was re-carved by none other than Lord Byron. Casanova died in 1798.

When will the twenty-first century begin?

Because our system of dating goes back to the year we suppose Christ to have been born, AD1 (there being no year AD0), the new century will begin on 1 January 2001. The last day of the twentieth century will be 31 December 2000.

Has the mystery of the Charfield children been resolved?

At 5.20 on the morning of 13 October 1928, the night mail train from Gloucester to Bristol ran into the back of a goods train that was reversing into a siding. It was a terrible crash: the mail train caught fire and 17 people died. The mystery arose because of speculation that two unaccompanied children, who were travelling on the train and were killed, were never claimed.

The man in the ticket office thought he remembered selling tickets to two children of about seven to nine years of age. They were wearing school uniforms and appeared to be travelling alone. In the wreckage of the crash, two pairs of children's shoes were found bearing the name G.S.S. Saunders. They were never claimed and the pairs of shoes and some ashes were subsequently buried at Charfield and the inscription reads, 'Two Unknowns.'

The story was further complicated by the fact that two children had been travelling with their mother on the train but they survived and neither had lost shoes. The name G.S.S. Saunders did not yield any further information. And so the mystery remains.

Who was the original **chauvinist**?

Chauvinism comes from the French soldier Nicholas Chauvin who served under Napoleon in the nineteenth century. He was a simple-minded soul who served his country faithfully, was wounded several times and received only a small pension for his troubles. This unthinking patriotism came to be ridiculed in the popular entertainment of the 1830s and his name came forever to be linked with smug, irrational belief in one's country, party or sex.

Why do eggs contain such high levels of **cholesterol** when chicken meat is relatively free from it?

Eggs contain the highest cholesterol content of commonly eaten foods (brains contain an even higher level). Cholesterol is present in eggs to nourish the foetus and aid the development of the chick before it leaves the egg, but it does not continue to be a significant element in the meat after the chick is hatched.

Is **chop suey** a traditional Chinese dish?

The ingredients are regularly found in Chinese kitchens: bean sprouts, bamboo shoots, water chestnuts, rice, soy sauce and a few bits of meat or fish. The name is Chinese (Cantonese), meaning 'odds and ends', but the dish is pure American. To quote from the *Rochester Post-Express* of 8 June 1904 (one of the first references): 'One of the Chinese merchants

of New York ... explained that *chop suey* is really an American dish, not known in China, but believed by Americans to be the one great national dish of the Celestials.'

What was the **Civil Air Guard**?

It was started on 1 September 1938 by the Under Secretary of State, Harold Balfour. Its aim was to encourage civilian interest in flying at a time when war was approaching by offering flying lessons at a very reasonable cost. (We were told by our questioner that she was charged two shillings and sixpence (12½p) per lesson at Gatwick.) By June 1939 some 3500 people were having flying lessons and many of those joined the RAF or Fleet Air Arm when war was declared in September of that year. The scheme was abandoned and never reinstated, partly because the increased cost of flying made it too expensive.

Are **clergymen** not banned from standing for Parliament? If so what is the Rev. Ian Paisley doing in the Commons?

Among those ineligible to stand for Parliament are clergy of the Churches of England, Ireland and Scotland and the Roman Catholic Church. Ian Paisley is a minister of the Martyrs' Memorial Free Presbyterian Church of Ulster which does not fall into any of those categories.

What is the material known as **Cloth of Gold** made from?

Threads, wires or strips of gold are interspersed with silk or wool to produce the richest of all fabrics. There are descriptions in the Bible of people wearing Cloth of Gold. Chaucer refers to it in a wall–hanging and in 1520, when Henry VIII met Francis I of France outside Calais, so magnificent were the robes and so lavish the entertainment that it became known as the Field of the Cloth of Gold.

Which country has the longest **coastline**?

Canada, with 56 453 miles (90 833 km) – a long way ahead of its nearest rival Indonesia, with 34 000 miles (54 706 km). Britain's coastline is 4928 miles (7929 km) and the country with the shortest coastline is Monaco at 3½ miles (5.6 km)!

Do the **cockroaches** that infest many kitchens have any predators?

When we think of cockroaches, we normally think only of the one species that has become a household pest. But there are about 3500 species that live blameless lives elsewhere. The cockroach forms an essential part of the food chain and is eaten by many other creatures.

But does the domestic cockroach have any predators? Yes, mice. So a plague of cockroaches or mice – the choice is yours!

Why are one- and two-pence coins minted
after 1992 attracted to magnets?

Why are one- and two-pence **coins** minted after 1992 attracted to magnets?

Not – you won't be surprised to hear – to make them easier to retrieve from down the side of the sofa! The Royal Mint switched from making the coins from bronze to copper-plated steel in 1992 because they had become more expensive to produce than their face value.

What are the most popular **colours** for cars?

Blue and grey, because those are the colours favoured by fleet owners. Among private buyers the two most popular are red and white. The least popular appears to be green which is said to be unlucky. This is an old superstition that probably dates from the time when Britain was greener than it is now. It was speculated that green cars were less visible and so involved in more accidents.

Did Sir Arthur **Conan Doyle** introduce skiing to the Swiss in 1893?

This sounds a bit like selling sand to the Arabs or refrigerators to the Eskimos (sorry Inuits). We can only quote Sir Arthur's words. In his autobiography, *Memories and Adventures*, he wrote: 'I think I have been able to do some practical good for I can claim to have been the first to introduce skis into the Grisons division of Switzerland ... or at least to demonstrate their practical utility as a means of getting across in winter from one valley to another.' He had seen skiing in

Norway and imported a pair of Norwegian skis into Switzerland for his demonstration, watched by the Swiss, he says, with 'innocent amusement'. As the Grisons region of Switzerland includes resorts such as Klosters, Davos and St Moritz, Sir Arthur has some justification for his claim.

What happened to Concordski, the Soviet version of the Anglo-French supersonic airliner Concorde?

Concorde first flew on 2 March 1969 and went into service on 21 January 1976 as the world's first supersonic passenger plane. The Soviet TU-144 was developed at much the same time and had many design similarities, which caused it to be dubbed Concordski. However, it never achieved supersonic speeds and in 1973 one of the prototypes crashed at the Paris Air Show. The project never fully recovered. It was used on internal freight-carrying flights and, briefly, for conveying passengers. Rumours of another crash were denied. Then, in 1984, the Soviets announced that Concordski would fly no more because it was too expensive to operate.

When did conducting prove to be a fatal occupation?

The Italian composer Jean Baptiste Lully, who lived in France, was conducting a *Te Deum* for the recovery from illness of King Louis XIV and thumping out the rhythm on the floor with a long cane. Unfortunately, on a particularly vigorous downbeat, he hit his foot and an ulcer developed from which he died. The King survived and lived a further twenty-five years.

How was Wellington almost beaten by **Copenhagen**?

Wellington's horse at the Battle of Waterloo was called Copenhagen and he had carried the Duke through three previous battles. It was the grandson of Eclipse, one of the most famous racehorses of all time, which was unbeaten in eighteen races between May 1769 and October 1770 and is still in the record books. After the battle, Wellington returned Copenhagen to his stalls, patted him on the rump and narrowly missed being injured by its flying hooves as the horse lashed out. How would that have looked in the record books? To have survived the battle unscathed only to be kicked to death by his horse!

Is there a legal maximum to the amount of **coppers** a shopkeeper is obliged to accept?

The Royal Mint and the Bank of England have set legal limits on the amount of coins you are obliged to accept: 20p in coppers, £5 in 5p and 10p pieces and £10 in 20p and 50p pieces. However there is no restriction governing the £1 coin as the rules have not been amended since we had the £1 note. Therefore if somebody offered to buy your house for a van-load of coins you would be legally obliged to accept!

What is **corned beef**?

Corned is the Old English word for meat that has been cooked and preserved in salt or brine. Corned beef is boiled with salt, sometimes sugar and sodium nitrite which is a preservative but which also gives the meat its traditional pink colour. It is one of the oldest tinned foods, going back over a hundred years.

Corned or 'bully' beef was the staple diet of the troops in France during the First World War – 'bully' from the French word *bouillir*, to boil.

Is there any cream in **cream crackers**?

No, and there never has been. One essential ingredient is yeast, and cream of tartar (as in baking powder) was added to the dough to assist fermentation and improve the flavour. Nowadays yeast fermentation is more easily controlled so cream of tartar is no longer required. Its place has been taken by malt extract.

Why do England's **cricket** team wear the old King's crown on their sweaters rather than the present Queen's crown?

The two crowns differ in shape: the Queen's crown has shoulders at the sides whereas the King's crown is more the shape of a bishop's mitre. When the Queen came to the throne, most emblems bearing the crowns were changed, so why not the badge on the cricketer's sweater? It appears that the right to wear the 'Crown and Three Lions' was granted informally to cricketers by Edward VII whose great friend, Lord Dalmeny (later Lord Roseberry), was a well-known cricketer at the time. Footballers, by contrast, only wear the 'Three Lions' and cricketers only wear the crown emblem when playing at home. The crown emblem is not used as a Royal warrant but simply as a badge in a similar way to the use of the 'Prince of Wales Feathers' by the Welsh rugby team.

Who invented the **crisp**?

It all came about by accident. In 1853, the chef of the Moonlake Hotel in Saratoga Springs, New York State, was an American Indian chief with the unlikely name of George Crum. One day the steamship and rail baron Cornelius Vanderbilt was entertaining friends in the hotel restaurant and, dissatisfied with his food, sent it back to the kitchen. An exasperated Crum thinly sliced the potatoes, fried them, and returned them to the table. The result was an immediate success and for many years the humble crisp (chip in America) was solely a restaurant item.

It was ninety years before Britain took up the idea, thanks to the potato being one of the few foodstuffs not on ration at the end of the Second World War. The crisp industry in Britain today is worth some £86 million annually and employs around 10 000 persons.

What does the D in **D-Day** stand for?

D-Day and H-Hour are standard military expressions. They are necessary because operations such as the Normandy landings would be planned and discussed long before date and time were decided on. So, in advance, 6 June 1944 was referred to as D-Day and the term stuck.

Who laid out the numbers on the dartboard?

Who laid out the numbers on the dartboard?

Brian Ganlin, a carpenter from Bury, is the man credited with designing the standard dartboard. Although the layout of the numbers may look random, there is method in the madness. The laws of gravity make it likely that a player will shoot low rather than high so the double twenty, at the top of the board, is harder to get than the double three at the bottom. High numbers are also flanked by low numbers making a miss expensive. There are variations to this pattern such as those found on the Manchester, Ipswich and Yorkshire boards.

How were the Dead Sea Scrolls discovered?

By accident. In 1947, a shepherd boy was walking past a series of caves on the shores of the Dead Sea in Jordan and threw a stone into one of them. The noise of a breaking jar alerted his attention and the discovery was made.

Altogether about 500 different documents were discovered stored in similar jars in eleven caves. They include texts of many Old Testament books, books of prophecy and commentaries written in Hebrew and Aramaic and dating from around the second century BC. They are thought to have been the library of a Jewish sect called the Essenes.

Do sitting MPs have to put up a **deposit** at General Elections and if they win do they get it back? What happens to lost deposits?

Everybody who stands for election to Parliament, whether or not they are seeking re-election, must pay the £500 deposit. If they achieve 5% or more of the vote, that deposit is returned. If they fail to get the required amount the money goes first to the Home Office Electoral Unit and then to the Treasury where it is added to the Consolidated Fund, the main purpose of which is to pay off the national debt. The 1992 General Election raised £440 022.80 in revenue from lost deposits. Why such an odd amount when everybody is required to pay £500? Administration costs!

Why is the **Deputy Speaker** in the chair in the House of Commons for the budget speech which is surely one of the most important Commons' events of the year?

Until 1967, what was taking place when the Chancellor presented his budget speech was a meeting of the Ways and Means Committee, traditionally chaired by the Deputy Speaker. Because so many MPs wished to attend, it was held in the Chamber instead of a committee room. Since 1967, the budget is presented to the House as a whole, but the tradition of the Deputy Speaker has continued.

How did the southern states of America come to be called Dixie?

As the books say, 'origin obscure', but there are two main theories. Firstly, the boundary between the 'slave' states in the south and the 'free' states in the north was surveyed in the eighteenth century by two Britons, Charles Mason and Jeremiah Dixon, and came to be known as the Mason-Dixon Line – hence Dixie. Secondly, on the $10 bill issued by the Bank of New Orleans, which was largely French speaking, was the word *dix* (French for ten), giving rise to the land of the 'Dixies'. Take your pick!

What is the origin of the dollar sign?

The Spanish Imperial coinage of the eighteenth century was the *real*, the most famous being the silver eight *real* or 'piece of eight' as immortalized in pirate tales. Although in use in the Americas, the coins were minted in Spain and showed a scroll with two pillars symbolizing the Pillars of Hercules (the mythical name for the Straits of Gibraltar). Gradually, when written, the symbol came to be the familiar S with the two vertical lines that we recognize today.

We know who lives at numbers 10 and 11 Downing Street. What about numbers 1 to 9?

There are only three numbered houses in Downing Street: 10, 11 and 12. Number 12 is the Government Chief Whip's house but unlike 10 and 11, where the Prime Minister and the Chancellor live and work, number 12 operates only as an office. There have never been any houses numbered 1 to 9 in Downing Street.

Until the eighteenth century there was a brewery on the site which was demolished to create the street, named after the English statesman Sir George Downing.

We say somebody's 'ears are burning' when they are being spoken about. Is it an old saying?

At least as old as Shakespeare and also known to the ancient Romans. Pliny talked of the Roman belief that if your left ear tingles somebody is speaking ill of you, but if your right ear tingles you are being praised. A small Mercury-like god was said to be always around waiting to tweak an ear. In the Netherlands they have the same superstition but have a way of combating it: if your left ear itches, bite your little finger and the slanderer will bite his own tongue.

Why do my ears pop in an aircraft even though it is pressurized?

Because the cabin of an aircraft is not pressurized to the equivalent of atmospheric pressure at ground level: 15lbs per square inch.

The higher an aircraft flies, the lower the pressure outside. If ground-level pressure were to be maintained inside the cabin, the internal stress on the aircraft would be greatly increased. This would mean strengthening it further, thus adding to its weight and operating costs. So it is a compromise between maintaining a relatively comfortable cabin atmosphere while keeping the aircraft as light as possible.

But why is the pressure change more noticeable on landing than on take off? Because on the ascent the air in the middle ear can escape relatively easily via the Eustachian tubes, but on descent the air has to be forced back into the ear which is more difficult and can cause some discomfort.

If the centre of the earth is hot, why is it that water drawn from a 150-foot borehole is cold?

A 150-foot (50-metre) borehole is not deep enough to find a rise in the earth's temperature. The deeper you go from the earth's surface the less effect the heat of the sun will have, but between 200–300 feet (60–100 metres) things start to warm up. At that depth water temperature is about 20° Celsius (approximately 68° Fahrenheit) and at a mile really hot water is found, such as comes to the surface at Bath. When you get to about three miles down water reaches boiling point.

Why is Easter a moveable feast when Christmas Day is always 25 December?

The original festival celebrated by the early Christians was the Jewish feast of the Passover, which was the day on which Jesus Christ died. That day fell on 14 Nisan according to the Jewish calendar. Nisan is the first month of the Jewish year and begins with the first appearance of the new moon. Thus

14 Nisan always came at full moon and the celebration was moveable according to the phase of the moon.

In later years, some wanted to observe Jesus' death on a fixed day but others felt it more important to commemorate his resurrection and as Jesus was resurrected on a Sunday that day, in time, became the permanent day of celebration. The church then adopted Easter, the pagan celebration of rebirth, as the occasion to mark.

How the date of Easter should be determined was a hot issue in the fifth century. Rome favoured one method and Constantinople another. The controversy rumbled on for 500 years until, in 1054, the eastern countries broke away in the Great Schism and formed the Orthodox Church which celebrates Easter according to its own calendar. In the Latin Church, the date of Easter is dependent on the phase of the moon, being the first Sunday after the first full moon after the Vernal Equinox. So it will always fall between 22 March and 25 April.

The book of Common Prayer, first published in 1622, contains the calculation for the dates of Easter through to the year 2299.

Can **eggs** be too fresh?

Very fresh eggs can be difficult to peel when hard boiled. This is because with new laid eggs the shell, the inner membrane and the egg itself are all packed tightly together. But with age a small amount of shrinkage takes place making them easier to peel. Very fresh eggs are best kept in a fridge for about a week before boiling. However, don't keep them too long: the older they are, the runnier the white and the flabbier the yolk. For poaching and frying, the fresher the eggs the better.

What did Albert **Einstein** receive his Nobel Prize for?

Not, as you would expect, directly for his theories on Relativity. So revolutionary were those ideas that many of his seniors in the scientific world were suspicious of them. His Nobel Prize of 1921 was given for his work on the Photoelectric Effect.

How does an aircraft's **ejection seat** work?

Very cleverly! The seat in which the pilot normally sits in an emergency ejects itself, and the occupant, away from the aircraft so that he can parachute to safety. To operate the seat, the pilot pulls a handle and fires a cartridge which does three things: it tightens his shoulder harness, pulling him back into his seat; it blows off the cockpit canopy; and it pressurizes the ejection gun which fires seat and pilot together out of the aircraft. As the seat moves, nylon chords pull back the pilot's legs and arms, holding them against his body and, at the same time, an oxygen supply is switched on. Once the ejection seat is about six feet clear of the aircraft, a rocket fires 4500lbs of thrust. If the pilot was on the ground he would be shot 300ft into the air. A small parachute is then deployed to stabilize man and seat and this, in turn, releases the main parachute. The seat then falls away, allowing the pilot to descend gently to earth. This remarkable invention is said to have saved nearly 6000 lives to date.

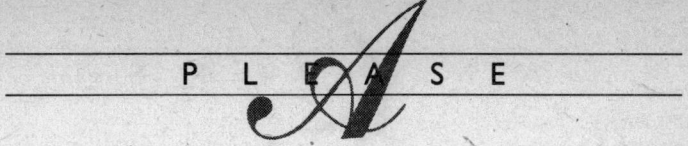
Could electrolysis be used to remove a man's beard and make it unnecessary for him to shave?

The technique of electrolysis involves sticking a fine needle into each hair follicle and passing an electric current into it to kill the hair root. It would be possible to eliminate a man's beard but it would take a very long time and so cost a fortune. Electrolysis is used on men, but in general only for small areas such as trimming bushy eyebrows.

Who was St Elvis?

The original St Elvis (in deference to the late King's legion of fans) was a sixth-century Celtic saint. One legend has it that he was left to die by his father but was suckled by a she-wolf; another that the patron saint of Wales, St David, was placed in the care of St Elvis as a child. The name was originally spelt Ailbe (pronounced Álava), which became Alveus which, in turn, became Elvis.

Who was Eric the Red?

Eric the Red was an early Norse explorer who was banished from Norway as a child with his father who had committed manslaughter. He settled in Iceland before going on to colonize Greenland around 986 with Icelandic settlers. His son, Leif Eriksson, became the first European to discover America. Having been converted to Christianity by King

Olaf I, he set out for Norway to spread the word but went the wrong way. He landed in what he called Vinland – now known as Nova Scotia. (See also Douglas '**Wrong Way**' Corrigan.)

Why doesn't **ERNIE** produce the name of Premium Bond winners as well as numbers?

Because in 1956, when ERNIE (Electronic Random Number Indicator Equipment) started work, one of the conditions of the prize draw was that there would be no publicity for winners. Complete anonymity is assured.

Can you sell a fridge to an **Eskimo**?

Yes. A fridge is an insulated box that keeps food at a different temperature to that outside. Eskimos often buy fridges to keep their food from freezing. Incidentally, Inuit rather than Eskimo is the preferred word.

Which is more correct when writing a letter: to address a man as Mr Fred Sponge or Fred Sponge **Esquire**?

The title 'Esquire' was introduced by the Normans in the eleventh century and originally referred to an apprentice knight. Its use was broadened to include any Lord of the Manor but by the time of John of Gaunt, in the fourteenth century, even master cooks were being styled esquire. James I

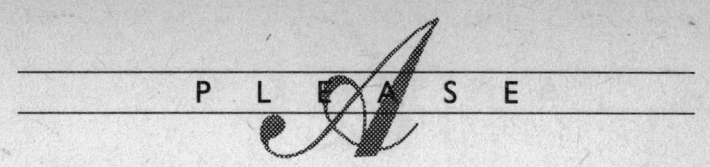

Can you sell a fridge to an Eskimo?

tried to restrict the use of the title without much effect and, nearer to our own time, it became common practice to use the title when writing to professional men such as lawyers or architects. Debrett's, the authority on all such things, now say that Mr and Esq. are completely interchangeable but Esq. is being used less and less.

When and where did the **Eurovision** Song Contest start?

Lugano, Switzerland, in 1956 and Britain did not take part. The *Concours Eurovision de la Chanson* came about with the birth of Eurovision (the Network of the Broadcasting Union for the exchange of news and television programmes). Countries were eager to have an international event to test the technology and the first winner was appropriately the home country, Switzerland, with a song called 'Refrains'.

What is the secret of **Fatima**?

Only two people know the secret of Fatima: the Pope and an old lady called Lucy.

Between May and October 1917 three children, Lucy being one of them, reported seeing repeated visions of the Virgin Mary at the town of Fatima which lies north of Lisbon in Portugal. She is said to have appeared to them six times and told Lucy two secrets which she was instructed never to divulge. The Pope is said to have been told and it is presumed he passed them on to his successors. Lucy now lives in a strict Carmelite convent.

It is rumoured that the first secret was a prophecy of the 1939–45 war and the second was a warning of a similar catastrophe to come. Fatima has since become a place of pilgrimage.

What were the **Fifies**?

It was the name given to the ferries that used to ply backwards and forwards across the River Tay between Dundee and Fife. There were five of them: the *Abercraig*, *Scottscraig*, *B.L. Nairn*, *Sevillian High* and *Newport*. The service started in 1824 between Broughty Ferry and Tay Port and ended in 1966 with the building of the Tay Road Bridge.

In the Second World War we heard much of the German **Fifth Column**, but what was the Fourth Column?

The Fifth Column refers to traitors or those within a country working for the enemy and is a term which originated in the Spanish Civil War. When Franco's Nationalist forces were laying siege to Madrid in October 1936, General Mola claimed he had four columns of troops encircling the city plus the additional support of a fifth column of Franco supporters inside the city. The phrase caught on and was later used by the Germans.

Where does the expression 'a **flash in the pan**' come from?

Flintlock firearms had a pan that held the priming powder and, when the trigger was pulled, the hammer struck the flint producing a spark that ignited the priming powder which, in turn, set off the main charge in the breech. On occasion only the priming powder ignited, the main charge failed and the gun did not fire. Thus you had a 'flash in the pan': a short-lived brilliance with no result.

The **Flying Fortress** was one of the most famous bombers of the Second World War. So why do some say they were a failure?

The RAF wished to try high-altitude daylight bombing raids and, against the advice of the Americans, bought twenty B17c aircraft – Boeing Fortress Mk 1 as they were known here – and they were a disaster. Although capable of flying at 30 000 ft (9000 m), twenty-six of the fifty-one sorties flown had to be aborted and not a single bomb was dropped. There were many technical problems: the bomb sights were no good; there were too few guns and those they did have froze at altitude; and they had a blind spot under the tail which made them vulnerable to attack from the rear. The Flying Fortress was consequently taken out of service, the design was modified considerably and, when they returned (when the Americans entered the war), they went on to become a very successful aircraft.

Why, when somebody is in danger of being struck by a golf ball, does a golfer shout 'fore'?

Considering the age of the game this is a relative newcomer to the vocabulary of golf as it dates back only just over 100 years. It coincided with the introduction of the harder ball and probably comes from the word 'be-fore'. The shout has thankfully become synonymous with the ball approaching from any direction, including 'be-hind'!

We've been told that Britain is to have some new forests. How far has the project got?

In 1988, the Forestry Commission announced plans for three new forest projects and a further nine were announced eighteen months later. The aim is to convert former industrial land close to towns and cities into recreational areas and, although called 'forests' after the style of New Forest and Epping Forest, only about 30% of the land will be covered by trees.

The Commission also produced some surprising figures: at the turn of the century, only about 5% of Britain could be termed 'forest'. That figure is now 7.5% and, when the scheme is fully realized, it will rise to between 25% and 30%. There has been no forestation project on this scale in Britain since the writing of the Domesday Book.

Is it a myth that the painting of the **Forth Railway Bridge** is never-ending?

No, it's true. A team of twenty-five men is continually painting through the spring and summer. It takes just over four years to paint from end to end, at which point they start all over again. In all they use some 17 tons of paint to cover the 145 acres (59 hectares) of steelwork.

What are the **Frankin Days** and why are Devon folk reluctant to plant-out until they have passed?

Legend has it that a Devon brewer named Frankin discovered that the local cider makers were doing too well at the expense of his beer so he made a pact with the Devil. He sold his soul in return for three late frosts in May to kill off the apple blossom. The Frankin Days are 19, 20 and 21 May.

Who or what is **Fray Bentos**, as in corned beef?

It is neither a 'who' nor a 'what' but a 'where'. Fray Bentos is a port on the River Uruguay famous as a meat-packing centre and, particularly, for corned beef.

Why are the doors at the back of a house leading on to the garden known as **French doors** or windows?

Because they originated in France. A pair of fully glazed doors opening on to a veranda or garden was an innovation first used at the Palace of Versailles between 1665 and 1683.

What is French about **French polish**?

It was a French invention. Two brothers (some say cousins) called Martin developed the technique in France in the eighteenth century and it came to Britain in 1815 for use, initially, on pianos. It was not applied to furniture generally until the end of the nineteenth century. Previous polishes had been applied with a brush but French polishing called for shellac, dissolved in a spirit base, to be applied with a 'rubber' – a pad of cotton and wadding.

When was the last **Frost Fair** held on the Thames?

The Thames used to freeze much more regularly than it does now and in a particularly cold winter it would freeze over completely because the flow of water was impeded by the twenty piers of the old London Bridge.

The first Frost Fair is recorded in the winter of 1564–65 when all manner of entertainment took place on the ice including archery and dancing. In later years bull-baiting, horse racing and football were introduced. In 1683–84 it was even thick enough to allow an ox to be roasted.

The last Frost Fair was in 1813–14. Ten years later the old bridge was demolished and replaced by one which no longer held up the flow of the river.

Why do you need to defrost a **frozen chicken** before cooking, but not vegetables?

To kill harmful bacteria in food the temperature has to be raised above 70°C. The danger with cooking a frozen chicken is that, although the surface temperature may exceed 70°C, the heat may not penetrate to the centre of the meat. And if it does, the outside of the meat will be overcooked.

Unlike meat, vegetables do not harbour harmful bacteria internally. Although they may be present on the surface they are killed off the moment the vegetable is plunged into boiling water – the rest of the time is cooking time. The process of blanching should kill off external bacteria.

Why does **fruit** turn sour when cooked?

In addition to the natural sugars found inside the cells of fruit there are a number of what are termed 'organic acids': citrus, malic and tartaric are three of them. When fruit is eaten raw you do not taste these acids as they remain locked inside cells. But during cooking the cellular structure is broken down releasing the acids which overpower the natural sweetness of the fruit.

What is the origin of the phrase 'to run the gauntlet'?

It has nothing to do with gloves or armour. There was a military punishment in the seventeenth century known as 'running the gantlope' (from the Swedish *gata*, a way, and *loop*, passage or passageway) in which an offender was made to run between two ranks of soldiers who beat him with the ends of pieces of rope.

From gantlope has come gauntlet and the present meaning, 'to be under attack from all sides'.

When did the word gay come to mean homosexual?

The change started a surprisingly long time ago. Since the Middle Ages the word 'gay' has been associated with sexuality. In Provençal French it meant a 'loose woman' and it was commonly used in that sense in England in the sixteenth century. By the nineteenth century, 'to turn gay' meant 'to become a prostitute'. In America in the 1930s it started to be used to refer to male homosexuals. We imported that meaning in the middle 1950s and, to the annoyance of many, the 'merry' meaning of 'gay' has gone forever.

Who founded the Gideon Society;

The Gideon Society was founded in Jamesville, Wisconsin, in 1899 by three businessmen: Samuel Hill, William Knight and John Nicolson. It is best known for the Bibles it places in hotel bedrooms so that travellers should never be without something to read. The international headquarters is now in Nashville, Tennessee, and to date they have distributed well over seven million Bibles and 45 million New Testaments.

Was there a real person called **Gipsy Rose Lee**?

Lee is a very common name among gipsy families so there have been many gipsies called Rose Lee. The most famous of them all however was not really a Lee. Born Rose Louise Hovick in 1914 on the West Coast of America, she became the 'Queen of Burlesque' and perhaps the world's most famous striptease artiste. She later acted in films, wrote a couple of novels and her autobiography, *Gipsy* (1957), was made into a very successful musical. She died in 1970. The critic H. L. Mencken attempted to dignify Gipsy Rose Lee's profession by coining the word 'ecdysiast' – from the Greek *ekdusis*, 'stripping'. Miss Lee rewarded him for his efforts by saying: 'He must have been reading books.'

Does a **giraffe** lie down to sleep and, if so, what does it do with its neck?

There is a myth that giraffes never lie down, but they do. Another myth says they don't make noises, but they do that too. London Zoo's giraffes lie down, curl up nose-to-tail and fall into a deep sleep for about five hours a night. They also sleep or doze during the day standing up, but they like something to lean against for that!

What is the origin of the name Glasgow?

It comes from two Gaelic words: *glas* meaning green and *cau* meaning a hollow. So Glasgow was 'the place in the green hollow'.

How did army prisons come to be called 'the Glasshouse'?

One of the main detention centres built at Aldershot during the last war had a huge glass roof and became known as the Glasshouse. Since then the term has come to be applied to military prisons in general.

Which recording artist was the first to receive a gold disc for a million or more sales?

Glenn Miller in 1942 for 'Chatanooga Choo Choo'.

Who said 'There but for the Grace of God, goes God'?

It was said by Sir Winston Churchill about Sir Stafford Cripps who became Chancellor of the Exchequer in 1947 in the post-war government. Cripps introduced a number of austerity measures which made him unpopular and gave rise to Churchill's remarks. Churchill had a savage tongue at times – he also described the Prime Minister, Clement Attlee, as 'a modest little man with much to be modest about'.

In American films we hear of people being 'arraigned' before a **grand jury**. What is it?

In the American legal system, unlike in England, there are two types of jury: grand and petit. The petit jury is the equivalent of an English one in that twelve men or women who have taken the oath decide on a verdict in secret according to the evidence presented to them. In America both civil and criminal cases are heard by a petit jury whereas in England juries have almost disappeared from civil trials.

The grand jury in America consists of anything between twelve and twenty-three people whose job is to decide whether or not a case should go to court. They hear the evidence and decide on the probability of guilt. If the evidence is strong enough the case will continue. In England this task is carried out by the Crown Prosecution Service.

'I heard it through the **grapevine**.' Why grapevine?

The original Grapevine Telegraph was laid between Placerville and Virginia City in 1859. Instead of being supported on poles, the wires were attached to trees and fences or simply trailed along the ground. The sight resembled the fast-growing Californian vine, hence the name.

As a means of communication it was notoriously unreliable. Messages trusted to the Grapevine Telegraph were sometimes beaten to their destination by the Pony Express. Newspapers in California and Nevada took up the phrase and stories that were old or of dubious authenticity were referred to as having come 'through the grapevine'.

'I heard it through the grapevine.' Why grapevine?

When did the **Great War** end?

As all the world knows, 11 November 1918, Armistice Day, was when the fighting stopped, but that was not the end of the war. The talking began on 18 January 1919 at the Paris Peace Conference where the Allies and Americans discussed how Germany was to be punished and the future shape of Europe decided. This led to the Treaty of Versailles which was imposed on the Germans by the Allies but it was not agreed by the Americans who opposed the concept of the League of Nations. The end finally came on 31 August 1921 when American President Warren G. Harding signed a separate Peace Treaty with Germany and Austria.

What is the difference between **ground frost** and air frost?

The lower the temperature, the less moisture the air can hold. Hence, when the temperature drops below freezing the water comes out as frost. Ground frost occurs when the ground temperature falls below freezing. It rarely harms plants even though they may be covered in frost. Air frost occurs when the temperature at 1½ metres (5 feet) above ground falls below freezing and is much more damaging.

Where does the strange word haberdashery come from?

The Anglo Saxon word *habertas*, meaning small items of merchandise, came to include the heavy rough material needed to make the garments worn underneath suits of armour. A company was set up to provide this which later became the Worshipful Company of Habertas or Haberdashers which still exists today.

What makes our hair curl?

It all depends on the shape of the follicles – the tubes in the scalp in which the hair grows. If the follicle is straight, the hair will be straight; if bent, the hair will emerge with a curl. This fact is unalterable. However on very rare occasions, perhaps after a blow to the head, the follicles may be damaged resulting in an otherwise straight-haired person growing a patch of curly hair.

Why does a halo around the moon mean we should expect rain?

The moon's halo in an otherwise clear sky is caused by the refraction of its rays through a layer of very thin high cloud called cirrostratus which, unlike most clouds, are made up of ice crystals rather than water droplets. A warm front is often preceded by high clouds which thicken as low pressure approaches. It is therefore likely that rain will follow after a day or two.

Why is the abbreviation of Hampshire **Hants** and not Hamps?

Because the word being shortened is not Hampshire. The old name of the county was Hantunscir which means 'Southampton County'. Hampshire has only been in official use since 1959.

Why is the taking of three wickets with consecutive balls in cricket called a **hat-trick**?

Because traditionally a bowler who achieved the feat was awarded a new hat by his club. The record for the number of hat-tricks in a career is held by D. V. P. Parson of Kent with seven. On 22 May 1907, during his benefit match at Lords, A. E. Trott of Middlesex took four Somerset wickets with four consecutive balls and later in the same innings took a hat-trick.

Where does **helium** gas come from?

Strangely not from the atmosphere, but from underground. Helium is one of the products of radioactive decay and occurs in pockets in the earth's crust. 96% of the world's supply comes from America with the remaining 4% from Poland.

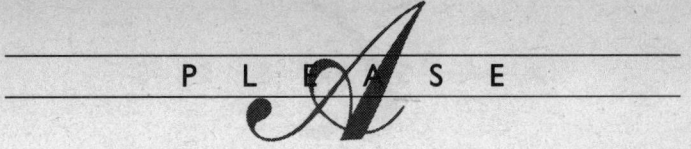

Why are American soldiers wearing British helmets in news-films of the attack on Pearl Harbor?

In the early years of the Second World War, before the Americans were involved, the US army was issued with helmets of a similar design to British ones, known as the 'soup plate'. By 1942 the design had been changed, so when their troops began to arrive in Europe they were all wearing the new helmet.

When did the term hit parade enter the language?

Lists of current songs available as sheet music were being published in the American trade paper *Billboard* as far back as 1913 but they were not given a rating. The first attempt to put the songs in some order of popularity based on sales came in the American radio programme *The Lucky Strike Hit Parade* which started on 20 April 1935 and ran until 29 April 1959, by which time the phrase had become part of the language. The first record chart appeared in *Billboard* on 20 July 1940 and, in Britain, on 14 November 1952 in the *New Musical Express*.

Was Adolf Hitler's real name Schickelgruber?

No, but it is an interesting story. Hitler's father was the illegitimate son of Maria Anna Schickelgruber and was named Allois Schickelgruber after his mother. She then married the boy's father, Johann Heidler, and it was Hitler's father who changed his name from Schickelgruber to Hitler (a variation of Heidler). Adolf Hitler was therefore born with that name but was repeatedly addressed as 'Herr Schickelgruber' by the American journalist Quentin Reynolds in a famous radio broadcast in 1941.

Some people have asked whether the course of world history would have been the same if Hitler had been born with his father's original name? 'Hcil Schickelgruber!' doesn't quite have the ring of 'Heil Hitler!'

What do the words **Hitum**, **Titum** or **Scrub** mean on an invitation to a social function?

You may well ask. It is doubtful whether they have been used on an invitation for fifty years. They were terms coined by the author, E. F. Benson in his *Mapp and Lucia* novels. Lucia used to divide dress into three classes: 'Hitum' was the very smartest and best, 'Titum' was moderately smart and 'Scrub' was casual – the sort of clothes worn on a picnic.

These stories of snobbery and intrigue became extremely popular with the smart set between the First and Second World War, hence the inclusion of the words on party invitations.

Who was Hobson of **Hobson's choice**?

Thomas Hobson was the owner of a livery stables in Cambridge that let out horses to university undergraduates and others. His clients were never given a choice of mount but his horses were offered in strict rotation. This inspired a contemporary writer to say of him: 'Every customer was alike, well served according to his chance, and every horse ridden with the same justice.' Hence, Hobson's choice is no choice at all – you take what you are given. For Thomas Hobson this was no bad thing: his business prospered and he died a very rich man in 1631 at a ripe old age.

Why does some **honey** set while other honey remains runny?

All honey will set, it is just a matter of how long it will take – in some cases it can take years. The rate of crystallization depends on the type of sugar and that, in turn, depends on the main flower the bees have been collecting from. Acacia honey is high in levulose and remains liquid for a long time whereas rape honey, which is high in dextrose, is the bane of some beekeepers' existence because it often sets before it can be removed from the comb. If heated all honeys become runny.

Conkers are also called **horse chestnuts**. Why 'horse'?

Because when the leaves fall, the scars left on the branch and the base of the leaf stem are horseshoe-shaped. And why 'conkers'? This is a corruption of 'conqueror' after the game played with them.

What were the names of the horses ridden by the film cowboys?

The Lone Ranger rode Silver and Tonto rode Scout.
The Cisco Kid rode Diabolo and Pancho rode Loco.
Gene Autry rode Champion.
Dale Evans rode Buttercup.
Roy Rogers rode Trigger.
Tom Mix rode Tony.
Kit Carson and Tex Ritter's horses were anonymous.

How severe was the hurricane that hit Britain in 1703?

There is no way of measuring it, but the storms did an immense amount of damage. Daniel Defoe wrote that they began on Wednesday 24 November and lasted about a week. People were afraid to go to bed for fear their houses would collapse around them – and many did. The Bishop of Bath and Wells was killed in his bed when the chimney fell in on him and in Kent 110 houses were destroyed. Eight thousand people also lost their lives in the floods when the Thames and Severn burst their banks. Sixteen thousand sheep were drowned in one place. The Eddystone Lighthouse was washed away and in London the damage was estimated at £2 million – an enormous sum of money in 1703. These extremely severe storms, which were described as a hurricane at the time, were said to be the worst ever recorded in England.

Why should the Prince of Wales bear the German motto **Ich Dien** on his crest?

An intriguing question – nobody knows for certain which Prince of Wales adopted the motto. Historians think it was probably Edward the Black Prince, son of Edward III, after the battle of Poitiers in 1356. Originally it was written *Ic Den*, old English for 'I serve', and this was later corrupted to the German *Ich Dien*.

Incidentally, the motto is found under the familiar three feathers which is usually referred to as the emblem of the Prince of Wales. Not so. It is the official emblem of the heir to the throne, so the present Prince was entitled to wear it prior to his investiture in 1969.

How did the village of **Indian Queens** in Cornwall get its name?

Surprisingly this derives from the American Indian woman Pocahontas who, according to the popular song 'Fever', had a mad affair with Captain Smith. She was not in fact a queen but the daughter of an Indian chief named Powhatan from Virginia in the early years of the seventeenth century. Captain John Smith was the leader of the English Community at Jamestown, which was on Indian territory, and when he was captured in 1607 he claimed it was Pocahontas who saved his life.

She later married the Englishman John Rolf who, in 1616, brought her, their son and about a dozen of the tribe to England where she caused a sensation. Taken for a princess, she was entertained at court but, just as she was preparing to leave the country, Pocahontas died from a fatal dose of smallpox. She was buried in St George's Churchyard, Greenwich. There is a suggestion, but no definite proof, that she and her entourage visited the West Country. Whether she did or not, several post houses are named after her, and one of these gave the name to the village of Indian Queens.

Why do we talk of an Indian summer?

A spell of warm sunny weather in early autumn is a feature of the New England climate. It is said that some eighteenth-century North American Indian tribes came to rely on it to complete their preparations for winter.

What do the inscriptions on the Welsh and Scottish £1 coins mean?

The inscription on the Welsh pound coin reads *Pleidiol Wyf I'm Gwlad* and means 'true am I to my country'. It is a line from the Welsh National Anthem.

The Scottish inscription *Nemo Me Impune Lacessit* translates 'none shall provoke me with impunity' and is a Latin proverb dating back to the Scottish battles with the Vikings.

The edge inscription written around the English £1 coin, *Decus Et Tutamen*, has been a tradition on coins since 1600 and means 'an ornament and a safeguard' and is a way of preventing the practice of 'clipping' gold and silver coins.

How many **insects** are there in the world?

You will not be surprised to hear that estimates vary, but when we are speaking of a figure approaching 10 to the power of 10, a few either way doesn't matter too much! Roughly speaking, there are a billion insects for every human being on the planet.

Who wrote the **Internationale**?

The words are by Eugene Pottier, the music by Pierre Degeyter. First sung in France in 1871, it was adopted as an international socialist anthem and was also the national anthem of the Soviet Union until 1943.

How do the **Inuit** get enough vitamin C?

Vitamin C is essential to health. The usual source is fruit and vegetables but these are unavailable for many months of the year in the frozen north. But vitamin C is also found in whale blubber and cod roe, as well as in the skin of the whale and the walrus, which the Inuit chew to such an extent they wear their teeth away! In the summer months the vitamin can be found in cloud berries, angelica and liquorice root.

Nowadays the Inuits, like the rest of us, get most of their vitamin C from the supermarket.

What is the highest **IQ** ever recorded?

The highest IQ we could find was 210, attained by a Korean boy named Kim. Born in 1963 to two professors he wrote poetry, spoke four languages and understood higher maths by the time he was four years and eight months old.

Why is the **Isle of Wight** so called?

The island has had several names. When first conquered by the Roman Vespasian in 44 AD, it was known as Vectis or Vecta meaning channel. Under the Anglo Saxon chief Cedric in 530 AD it was called Whitland – *whit* being the Saxon word for channel. The island became private property after the Norman Conquest but was bought back by Edward I in 1293 for 6000 marks when the name became Isle of Wight from the Celtic word *wyth* meaning – you guessed it! – channel.

What was the song that made **Ivor Novello** famous?

Ivor Novello began composing songs at the age of fifteen with some small success. Then in 1914, when he was 21, his mother suggested he wrote a patriotic song and even wrote a lyric for him called 'Keep the Flag a-flying'. This did not meet with approval but it started Novello on composing a melody. He then turned to a friend of his mother, the American poet Lena Guilbert Ford, who wrote the finished words of 'Keep the Homes Fires Burning'. This became one of the

What is the highest IQ ever recorded?

most popular songs of the First World War and made him a fortune.

Ned Sherrin in *In His Anecdotage* recalls that, during the Second World War, when Emlyn Williams heard that Novello faced imprisonment for an offence involving the wartime petrol ration, he said: 'I suppose the great song for this war will have to be "Keep the Home Tyres Turning".'

How much damage does **ivy** do to a tree?

Not being a parasite, ivy does not directly cause damage to a tree when climbing up it, using it for support rather than feeding. However it grows very vigorously and can be in competition with the tree for light and nutrients. It is therefore advisable to keep it in check.

Why are there so many Welsh surnames beginning with the letter **J** – Jones, Jenkins etc. – when there is no J in the Welsh language?

Because the language was spoken before it was written. The sound of a J was being used in England long before the letter was introduced in the sixteenth century. In the Welsh language they had the sound 'zh' (as in 'measure'), but as it was the English who introduced the idea of a surname to the Welsh they took the nearest equivalent letter which was a J.

The name **Jack Robinson** has passed into history but who was he?

A certain John Robinson was born in Appleby in the Lake District in 1727. He became mayor in 1760 before entering Parliament and becoming Secretary to the Treasury. The famous saying is said to have originated from a remark by the MP and playwright Sheridan. During a debate, he made allegations of bribery against the administration. Challenged to name the culprit, Sheridan looked hard at John Robinson and replied: 'Yes, I could name him as soon as I could say Jack Robinson.'

What did the **Jackdaw of Rheims** do to ensure its immortality?

He stole the Cardinal's ring. 'The Jackdaw of Rheims' is one of the Ingoldsby legends written by the Rev. Richard Harris Barham under the pseudonym Thomas Ingoldsby. They first appeared in *Bentley's Miscellany* and the *New Monthly Magazine* before being published in book form in 1840.

Who was **Jack-in-the-Green**?

Otherwise known as the Green Man, he was a central figure in British and European folk lore. His origins go back to pagan times when spirits were thought to live in trees (which is why some people still touch wood or knock on wood). He was then adopted by the early Christian church to represent resurrection and rebirth. He is usually portrayed as a man in the shape of a tree or looking out through a garland of leaves and is still found in church sculpture, wood carvings and pub signs.

What we used to call jam now seems to be called conserves or preserves. Is there any difference?

There shouldn't be!

To preserve is to keep from going off and the original reason for making jam was to preserve the fruit, so all jams are preserves. Conserve, in this context, has an old-fashioned meaning, 'to preserve in sugar'.

In practice there is a difference in fruit content. One manufacturer insists that conserves contain at least 45% fruit, preferably whole, compared to standard jam with 35% fruit.

When a building is constructed carelessly or with cheap materials we say it is jerry-built – why?

As is so often the case, the best explanation is also the incorrect one. Jerry sadly does not derive from Jericho whose walls came tumbling down at the blast of a trumpet! In this context jerry is a corruption of jury, the nautical term which refers to damage repaired at sea: you 'jury rig' a 'jury mast'. (Jury meaning temporary may derive from the French word *jour* – a day.) The first jerry-built houses are said to have been erected in Liverpool when speculators put up thousands of cheap homes to cope with the influx of immigrants from Ireland.

When was the first jet aircraft flown on active service?

The jet engine was patented in the UK by Sir Frank Whittle in 1930 and he made the first jet-powered flight in a specially constructed Gloster E28/39 on 15 May 1941. The first jet fighter to enter active service was the Gloster Meteor Mark 1, delivered to 616 squadron RAF on 12 July 1944, and first flown on active duty against the V-1 flying bombs (doodlebugs) on 27 July of that year.

Strangely, the first combat success by a jet-powered fighter came on 4 August 1944 when one Flying Officer Dean, after his guns had jammed, tipped a V-1 with the wing of his own aircraft and caused the bomb to crash.

Who was John Barleycorn whose effigy is immortalized on jugs?

John Barleycorn never really existed. He is the personification of liquor and also appears in Robert Burns' epic poem *Tam O'Shanter*:

> 'Inspiring bold John Barleycorn!
> What dangers thou canst make us scorn!'

Traditionally he was a squat old man in eighteenth-century clothes wearing a three-cornered hat, one corner of which formed the lip of the jug. However his predecessor, Toby of the Toby jug, may have been a real person. The Staffordshire potter Ralph Wood started making them in the 1760s and took his design from a contemporary print of a man called

Toby Philpott – a notoriously heavy drinker. Unfortunately nothing definite is known about Mr Philpott, so he too may have originated as a figure of fancy.

Why was **Joseph Schmidt** known as 'the Pocket Caruso'?

Because he was only 4' 10" in height but had a superb voice. Born in what is now Romania, he was too small for the opera but could, and did, make many films. The first was in 1931, *Der Liebesexpress*, in which he played a singing bartender. Being Jewish he fled from the Nazis into Switzerland, where he died in 1942 at the age of only thirty-eight. He is buried in Zürich and his headstone bears an inscription taken from the title of another of his films: *Ein Stern Fällt* – *A Star Fell*.

William **Joyce** (otherwise known as Lord Haw-Haw) who broadcast Nazi propaganda was executed at the end of the Second World War. But why, as an American, was he tried at the Old Bailey?

William Joyce was born in America to American parents. His father had become a naturalized American citizen and never renounced it, so when the family arrived in England they registered as aliens. However in 1933, when Joyce applied for a British passport, he lied about his nationality and claimed to be British. He did the same in 1938 and 1939 when he renewed his passport.

Joyce did not become a German citizen until September

1940 – after the outbreak of war. It was argued in court that, even though under American law he was entitled to change citizenship, by falsely claiming to be British to obtain a passport he had 'disavowed' himself of his American citizenship and thus sought 'the protection of the King'. The crime for which he was executed was that of taking German nationality when Britain at war with that country.

Who was St Jude who is so frequently thanked in the personal columns of the newspapers?

He was one of the twelve apostles and he has acquired the doubtful honour of being the patron saint of 'hopeless causes'. He was the other Judas, Judas Thadeus, perhaps the brother of James, which would have made him the half-brother of Jesus himself. Others say that he was James' son. According to tradition, he was martyred in Persia with his fellow apostle Simon whose feast day he shares (28 October). However because he was often confused with Judas Iscariot who betrayed Jesus, no one invoked his name. He therefore came to be regarded as the saint one turned to when all hope was lost.

Why is the jukebox so called?

From the juke houses, or brothels, in which they were originally found – which makes you wonder about the suitability of the British television programme *Jukebox jury* as family viewing! The word comes from the Gullah language.

Why hasn't the mountain K2 got a name like all the other famous peaks?

K2 was discovered and measured by the Himalayan surveyor Henry Godwin-Austen in 1856. It is in such a remote area that no local name could be found for it. General Walker, the Surveyor General of India, suggested it should be named after Godwin-Austen, which is its alternative name. But as it was the second peak to be measured in the Karakoram range it has always been known as K2.

At 28 500 feet (8686 m) K2 is the second highest mountain in the world. It was first climbed on 31 July 1954.

Under our Constitution if a King were to die leaving two daughters and a pregnant Queen, would the elder daughter succeed to the throne or would the succession be left until after the birth?

The throne would go into abeyance until the third child was born and a Council of State would be appointed to take the necessary decisions in the meantime. If the child were a boy, he would succeed to the throne. If a girl, the throne would pass to the eldest daughter. A Council of Regency or a single Regent would be appointed if necessary to undertake the monarch's decisions until the young King or Queen reached the age of 18.

Did the rank of **King's Corporal** ever exist?

This question is often asked and nobody knows why. The War Office, now the Ministry of Defence, made an exhaustive investigation in 1921 to establish whether or not such a rank existed but with no success. In 1944 Hansard records that a question was raised in the House of Commons about the numbers of King's Corporals and King's Sergeants, but again the War Office drew a blank.

It has been suggested that the confusion may have arisen from the term Kitchener's Sergeants which is what soldiers promoted in the field during the Boer War were called.

What was the **King's Evil**?

It was the disease known today as scrofula, a form of tuberculosis that causes ulcers to form, usually on the neck, and it was believed in the Middle Ages that only the touch of a sovereign could cure it. The earliest written references to the practice dates from 1387. Samuel Johnson was 'touched' by Queen Anne in 1714 and there was even a special office for the ceremony printed in *The Book of Common Prayer* until 1719.

What is the origin of the phrase 'to take a **kip**'?

It is not the innocent word it may seem. It comes from the early English word meaning a brothel which, in turn, came from the Danish *kippe* meaning a 'low alehouse'. From there it was applied first to a cheap lodging house, then just a bed and so it eventually came to mean 'to sleep'.

On his deathbed did Nelson say '**Kiss me Hardy**' or 'Kismet, Hardy'?

After being shot, Nelson was taken below decks where he lay in agony for three hours before dying. Because he was a national hero there were two or three people with him all the time and his every word was recorded, including the request that 'Poor Lady Hamilton', his mistress, be taken care of – a request later ignored by the government.

It is possible he uttered the words 'Kismet Hardy', but all those present thought he said 'Kiss me Hardy', including Hardy who kissed his Admiral and returned to the deck. Nelson is then reported to have said 'Now I am satisfied,' and died about twenty minutes later having issued the famous last words: 'Thank God I have done my duty.'

Why do **knees** and other joints crack?

The 'crack' is caused by what engineers call cavitation. As the surface of the joints move over each other, small unevennesses in the cartilage create tiny pockets of vacuum. This causes the moisture in the pockets to vaporize producing the strange explosive sound. The same effect can be noticed when a ship's propeller causes momentary cavitation in the water. The resulting explosion can damage the propeller's surface. For the same reason doctors are not too happy about people purposely cracking their joints!

What was the purpose of the **Kon-Tiki** voyage?

Thor Heyerdahl, the Norwegian ethnologist, wanted to prove that the pre-Inca peoples of South America could have crossed the Pacific ocean to Polynesia. With five companions (and a parrot which was washed overboard) he set out on 28 April 1947 on a balsa-wood raft named Kon-Tiki from Callao, Peru. He arrived in the Tuamotu Islands near Tahiti on 7 August 1947 after a journey of nearly 5 000 miles. Kon-Tiki was the name of an Inca god.

Was the **Kwanto** earthquake the worst ever recorded?

It depends on what you mean by worst because earthquakes are difficult to measure. Even the famous Richter scale (or Gutenberg-Richter scale, to give it its full name) is not considered satisfactory when the earthquake is felt over a large area. In such cases the Kanamori scale is used and the largest ever measured was the Lebu earthquake in Chile in 1960.

The highest death toll ever reported in an earthquake occurred in the eastern Mediterranean in 1201, with an estimated 1 100 000 fatalities. Better documented was the earthquake in the Shensi province of China on 2 February 1556 that killed 830 000 people. In modern times the highest death toll was at Tangshan in eastern China on 27 July 1976 when some 750 000 lives were lost.

The earthquake on the Kwanto plain of Japan in 1923 was the worst in terms of damage. It was estimated at the time to have cost £4 000 000 000 with 500 000 homes destroyed.

The highest death toll from an earthquake in Britain (yes,

they do happen!) is two. Thomas Grey, an apprentice, was struck on the head by masonry falling from Christ's Hospital Church, Newgate in London, on 6 April 1580 and Mabel Everet died of her injuries four days later.

Who was the Lady in White who sang to the troop ships entering and leaving Durban Harbour during the Second World War?

This question aroused a lot of interest because she was fondly remembered by many ex-servicemen. Her name was Perla Siedle Gibson, a singing pianist and portrait painter, whose self-imposed task was to greet every single troop ship entering and leaving Durban Harbour. More than 400 came and went between April 1940 and August 1945 and not one was missed – not even on the day Perla learned that her eldest son had been killed in action in Italy. Standing alone on the North Quay dressed in white she would sing 'Land of Hope and Glory' and other songs requested by troops on the ships that sailed by. Perla Gibson died in 1971.

Where does the word laser come from?

It is an acronym derived from Light Amplification by Stimulated Emission of Radiation.

Who was the Laughing Cavalier painted by Franz Hals?

The Laughing Cavalier is Franz Hals' most famous painting and is currently in the Wallace Collection in London. Nobody knows who he was – it could even be a self-portrait although the picture shows a younger man than the artist would have been at the time. The original title was simply *Portrait of a Man* but a newspaper review of 1872 called it *The Laughing Cavalier* and the name stuck.

Why do leaves change colour in the autumn?

The strange thing is they don't! Leaves look green during the spring and summer due to the presence of chlorophyll. When the leaf dies, the chlorophyll disappears revealing colours that were there all along.

Why is a church lectern so often in the form of an eagle with outstretched wings?

This is not the Imperial Roman Eagle but the eagle ascribed to St John. As writer of the fourth Gospel and the Book of Revelation, St John has been adopted by theologians, writers and all who work in the production of books as their patron saint. So to some it is appropriate that the Bible in a church should be opened on the wings of an outstretched eagle.

When was the first public **library** opened?

Several Roman and Byzantine emperors founded libraries to which the public had access and with the growth of Christian literature it became customary to attach libraries to churches. The first municipal public library in Britain was opened in Norwich in 1608. It was principally for members of the clergy and was eventually taken over by Norwich public library in 1857. All the 1772 original volumes are still together and form the oldest collection of books in the country available for public use.

Does anything travel faster than the speed of **light**?

We don't know. At approximately 186 000 miles per second (300 000 km per second) light has for a long time been regarded as the fastest thing in nature. However a mysterious event occurred in 1971. A celestial phenomenon from galaxy 3273 was calculated as travelling at three times the speed of light – which should be impossible.

Who discovered the speed of **light** and how was it measured?

In classical time astronomers believed the speed of light to be infinite and it was not until 1675 that an attempt was made to measure it. The Danish astronomer Ole Roemer noticed that the moons of Jupiter did not behave consistently and were not always where they were expected to be. He guessed this

Who discovered the speed of light and how was it measured?

had nothing to do with the moons themselves but was caused by changes in the distance between Jupiter and the Earth and so in the distance light had to travel. Using simple maths (as they always say!) he was able to estimate the speed of light at about 137 000 miles per second. He was slightly out – the speed of light in a vacuum is approximately 186 000 miles per second.

How many American soldiers died at the battle of **Little Big Horn**?

This battle, also known as Custer's Last Stand, was fought on 25 June 1876 on the south bank of the Little Big Horn river in Montana. General Custer disobeyed the orders of General Terry whose plan was to make a two-pronged attack on the Sioux Indians led by Sitting Bull and Crazy Horse. Custer went ahead on his own and rode into a massacre: all 266 men, including Custer, were killed. The only survivor was an army horse named Comanche.

What is the origin of the **Liver bird** so beloved by Scousers?

It probably came from lava bird, another name for the cormorant, which often inhabit ports like Liverpool. The bird is now the city's symbol and is on its crest. The most famous pair can be seen on top of the Liver Building on Pier Head and are one of the city's landmarks.

What is the origin of the name Liverpool?

Nobody really knows, but 'pool' on the end of a place name usually means a settlement on a tidal stream. 'Liver' could derive from the Old English *lifrig* (or, in Middle English, livered) meaning 'coagulated or clotted'. Liverpool is therefore 'a city on a pool of thick or turgid water' – charming!

Lobsters in America seem much bigger than ours. Is that true or are they just older?

There are two species of lobster: the American (*Homarus americanus*) and the European (*Homarus vulgaris*) and the American species is the larger. The record to date is held by a monster caught on 11 February 1977 off Nova Scotia that weighed 44 lbs 6 ozs (20 kg) and measured 3 ft 6 ins (1.07m) from claw to tail. The heaviest European lobster by contrast was caught in June 1931 and weighed a mere 20 lbs 8 ozs (9.3 kg). There is no simple way of knowing the age of a lobster but the largest of the American species could be up to fifty years old.

Where does the expression 'at loggerheads' come from?

It goes back to sixteenth-century naval warfare. A loggerhead was a long-handled ladle in which tar or pitch was melted before being hurled or dumped on the opponents alongside. When both crews were engaged in the practice they most certainly were 'at loggerheads'.

What is the origin of the expression 'It's all Lombard Street to a China orange'?

In the nineteenth century, Lombard Street in the City of London became famous as the home of many banks and insurance companies. It was a time when thousands of wild sweet-tasting oranges were being imported from China and sold cheaply. So, 'It's all Lombard Street to a China orange' meant it was very long odds – a million to one that something would happen.

'It's all Lombard Street to an eggshell' was a variation, while in America they said 'I'll lay dollars to a doughnut'.

What is the origin of the word London?

London's Latin name, Londinium, is thought to have derived from the Old Irish word *lond* meaning 'wild or bold'. Or possibly the city was named after a prominent Roman called Londinus.

How long is the longest day?

It depends on where you live:
In London, 16½ hours.
In Stockholm, 18½ hours.
In Tornio, Finland, 22 hours.
In Spitsbergen, 3½ months!

What happened to the **Lyons** shops?

Lyons Catering first appeared in 1887 at Queen Victoria's Jubilee Exhibition and the first Lyons Tea Shops, where you would be served by a 'Nippy' and where you could sit all day over a cup of tea and a twopenny bun, opened in 1894. Eventually there were 200 around London plus another 40 or 50 in other parts of the country. In addition there were four Lyons Corner Houses (large multiple restaurants on three or four floors).

Lyons Tea Shops were the 'fast food' cafés of the day but even faster cafés were destined to take over and the last one in London's Strand closed in 1988.

What is the story behind the Second World War bomber **McRobert's Reply**'?

Lady McRobert lost three sons: one shortly before the war in a flying accident and two during combat. In 1941 she gave the Air Ministry £25 000 for the purchase of a Short Sterling bomber Mk 1 – the first four-engined monoplane bomber to go into active service with the RAF. Named 'McRobert's Reply', it bore the family crest and flew on active service with 15 Squadron before being retired to training duty. The following year Lady McRobert gave a further £25 000 for the purchase of four Hurricanes for 94 Squadron which were named Sir Ian, Sir Roderick, Sir Alistair and the Lady. Her generosity extended still further when, in 1943, the family home, Alastrean House in Aberdeenshire, was put in trust for the RAF. It is still used today as a residential home for the elderly.

Magna Carta, 1215, is one of the major dates of English history. So what was the Magna Carta of 1225 signed by Henry III?

The original Magna Carta was signed at Runnymede in 1215 by King John and opens with this declaration: 'John by the Grace of God, King of England, Lord of Ireland, Duke of Normandy and Aquitaine, Count of Anjou to the archbishops, bishops, abbots, earls, barons, justices, foresters, sheriffs, stewards, servants and to all bailiffs and faithful subjects, greetings.'

It recognized the rights and privileges of the barons and confirmed the freedom of the Church and freemen and was an early statement of civil rights. However it was not universally welcomed. The Pope annulled the charter but it was revised in 1216 and 1217. By 1225, John's son Henry III was on the throne and he reissued it with some ceremony to celebrate his coming of age.

What is the **magpie** rhyme?

Birds have always had a special place in folk lore and because of their ability to fly it was believed they could see into the future. The magpie was particularly favoured because it is said to bring the news to the other birds with its characteristic warning shriek.

There are many variations of the magpie rhyme but this one comes from Scotland:

One for sorrow,
Two for mirth,
Three for a wedding,
Four for a birth,
Five for a christening,
Six for a dearth,
Seven is a heaven,
Eight is a hell,
Nine is the devil his ain sel' [own self].

One unsavoury custom meant to counteract seeing an 'unlucky' number of the birds is to spit three times!

Is there any connection between **Maida Vale** in London and Maida in Italy?

During the Napoleonic Wars, France was worried that the British might establish a base in Calabria and liberate Italy. So they ousted King Ferdinand IV from the throne and installed his brother, Joseph, in his place. This prompted a landing of 5000 British troops who fought and won the battle of Maida on 4 July 1806. The victorious troops were led by General Sir John Stewart and, soon after the battle, a pub was opened in his honour on London's Edgware Road. It was called 'The Hero of Maida Inn' from which came first Maida Hill and then Maida Vale.

What is the origin of the word **Manchester**?

The original Old English name was Mamucion. The Romans later built a camp there and the Latin for camp is *castra* which, in Old English, became *ceastra*. So Manchester is 'a camp at Mamucion'.

What is the **Manx Oath**?

It is the oath taken by the Deemster, one of two justices in the Isle of Man. The earliest recorded use of the oath was in 1609 although there are records of Deemsters being appointed 200 years before that.

The oath is sworn on the Bible as follows:

'By this Book and by the Holy contents thereof and by the wonderful works that God hath miraculously wrought in heaven above and in earth beneath in six days and seven nights, I [name] do swear that I will without respect of favour or friendship, love or gain, consanguinity or affinity, envy or malice, execute the laws of this Isle justly, betwixt our sovereign lady the Queen and her subjects within this Isle, and betwixt party and party as indifferent as the herringbone doth lie in the midst of the fish. So help me God and by the contents of this book.'

Why is the name **Maria** given to men in Spain, such as golfer José Maria Canazares?

In Catholic countries the name Maria is given to children of either sex in honour of the Virgin Mary. However, when applied to a girl the Spanish spelling is written with an accent on the final 'a' – (Mariá). It is also sometimes chosen after the name of the church the child is baptized in.

Did **Marie Antoinette** really say 'Let them eat cake'?

It is possible she said it, or something similar, but what is quite definite is that she did not originate it. It had appeared several times in previous centuries: John Peckham, Archbishop of Canterbury, quoted it in the thirteenth century; it was attributed to Marie Thérèse, wife of King Louis XIV, as 'Why don't they eat brioche?' and she died in 1683; Rousseau, in his *Confessions*, quotes it as a well-known saying and he was writing in 1740, some fifteen years before Marie Antoinette was born. The mystery is why history should wish to brand the unfortunate Queen of France, who died in the French Revolution, as such a heartless creature.

Why is **marmalade** not simply called orange jam or conserve?

There is a story that marmalade was first made by Mary Queen of Scots' French doctor as a cure for seasickness, hence *mer malade*. Much more likely is that it got its name from the Portuguese *mermelada*, a stiff paste made from oranges and quinces.

Marmalade as we know it today originated from Scotland. James Keiller of Dundee bought a cargo of oranges from Seville but found they were too bitter to use and his wife, Janet Pierson, decided to experiment. She made an orange jam which was so successful, that in 1797, Keiller & Son was established to make and market it.

Manufacture began in England in 1874 when Sarah Jane, wife of Oxford grocer Frank Cooper, began making it in the kitchens of the Angel Hotel from a family recipe. The dons called it 'squish' and so great was the demand that the local newspapers were soon hailing Oxford marmalade as one of the city's attractions.

Why was the word mayday chosen as the international distress call for ships and aircraft?

The word is not really 'mayday' but '*m'aider*', the French for help me. Its use dates back to 1907 when ships were being equipped with radio telephones. French was one of the languages in which the regulations were written and m'aider or mayday was chosen as the distress call because it was easily remembered and repeated.

What is the temperature on the planet Mercury?

Mercury is the planet closest to the sun, a mere 58 000 000 km away from it. Its daytime temperature rises to 327°C falling at night to −183°C! However, even though it is further away, thanks to its greenhouse effect the temperature on Venus can reach 464°C.

What is the difference between a meteor, a meteoroid and a meteorite?

All natural debris in space of whatever shape is a meteoroid. When a particle enters the earth's atmosphere and burns up we see it as a meteor or shooting star – and a grain of dust no larger than a mustard seed can produce a very respectable meteor. If the particle is large enough to come through the atmosphere and hit the earth it is called a meteorite. The largest found so far is at Hoba near Grootfontein in South West Africa. It measures roughly 8 × 9 ft (2.5 × 3 m) and weighs around 59 tons.

What age was Methuselah?

According to Genesis Chpt. 5:27 Methuselah, the grandfather of Noah, lived for 969 years. Some other long-livers in the Bible are Jared (962 years), Noah (950 years), Seth (912 years), Kenan (910 years), Enosh (905 years) and Mahalalel (895 years).

It was also customary among some other nations in biblical times to attribute great age to their ancient worthies on the principle that the longer you lived, the more wisdom you amassed. There is a list of eight Sumerian kings who together reigned for 241 000 years, or approximately 30 000 years each!

Who decided on the length we know as the metre and how was that length arrived at?

It is one 10 millionth of the distance from the North Pole to the Equator measured through Paris. The French abbot and astronomer Nicholas Louis de Lacaille made the calculation in 1740 and it was adopted by the revolutionary National Assembly in 1791, who were keen to do away with all things relating to the old order. The standard metre is now kept at the International Bureau of Weights and Measures in Paris and is the distance between two marks on a platinum-iridium bar.

However this did not satisfy modern scientists. The metre for a time was defined as 'equal to 1.650 763 73 wavelengths of the radiation emitted by a Krypton-86 atom in a specified transition'. Today that has been replaced by 'the length of the path travelled by light in free space during a time interval of 1/299 792 458 of a second'.

'Have you read him his Mirandas?' is a phrase used by American police. What does it mean?

It simply means 'Have you read him his rights?' In 1966, Ernesto Miranda was convicted of kidnap and rape in the US Supreme Court but the finding was later reversed by what was called the Warren Court. Chief Justice Earl Warren was concerned about the method police were using to obtain confessions, so the court that bore his name was set up to investigate a number of cases. He instituted a series of procedures intended to ensure that a suspect did not incriminate himself, which included informing him that he had the right to remain silent, but that anything he did say might be used in evidence against him. This became known as the Miranda Warnings.

When does the **Mistral** blow and do winds affect our health and state of mind?

The Mistral is a north or north-westerly wind that blows off the land along the north coast of the Mediterranean. It is at its strongest in Languedoc, Provence, and at the southern end of the Rhône Valley where it is funnelled between the Alps and the Massif Central. The Mistral is at its most dangerous in winter and spring when it can blow continuously for several days reaching speeds of 8/9 (gale and severe gale force) on the Beaufort Scale.

Many countries have similar named winds: the Santa Anna in California, the Foehn in Austria, the Chinook in the Rockies and the Sirocco in Italy. All are regarded as 'ill winds that blow no good'. There is some support for this idea. Biometrologists say winds can produce an excess of positive ions in the atmosphere which, some say, can cause irritability, headaches and other such symptoms.

Why are cats called **moggies**?

'Moggy', as a pet name for calves, is recorded in Cheshire, Warwickshire, Shropshire, Herefordshire and Gloucestershire. In Herefordshire a 'moggy' can also be a donkey, but only at the end of the last century was the term applied to cats, possibly by London Cockneys.

Where do the Mormons get their name from?

From the prophet Mormon who is said to have written the Book of Mormon.

The sect was founded in 1830 by Joseph Smith who claimed to have had a series of visions which culminated in the discovery of the golden tablets that contained the Book of Mormon. He said he had found them buried on a hillside near his home. They purported to be a record of early American history and religion and identified the American Indians with the ten lost tribes of Israel. Sadly for posterity the angel Moroni, who first enabled Smith to find the tablets, is said to have taken them back to heaven.

Joseph Smith was murdered by the mob in 1844 and in 1847 the persecuted Mormons, under their new leader Brigham Young, moved to Salt Lake City where they still have their headquarters.

The folk dancers of Old England are called Morris dancers. Who was Morris?

He wasn't! Morris is a corruption of 'Moorish' and the dances are said to have been introduced to England by John of Gaunt from north Africa around 1350. Nowadays a Morris team is usually twelve men, but in earlier times it was five men and a boy. The men danced as characters from the Robin Hood legend and the boy represented Maid Marian.

Why do moths fly into a candle flame?

Why do **moths** fly into a candle flame?

Moths and other insects navigate by the light from the sun and the moon. Because they are so far away, the light rays are almost parallel when they reach the earth and the insect flies in a straight line by keeping the light falling on its eye at a constant angle. In trying to do the same with a nearby light source, such as a candle, the moth flies around in circles getting ever closer until it spirals into the flame.

Who are the American Presidents whose faces are carved into **Mount Rushmore**?

They are George Washington, Thomas Jefferson, Abraham Lincoln and Theodore Roosevelt. Mount Rushmore is in the Black Hills of South Dakota and the monument to American freedom was the suggestion of Mr Doane Robinson, director of the South Dakota Historical Society, in 1923. The designer and sculptor was the unusually named John Gutzon de la Mothe Borglum, who accepted the commission in 1925 while on the run from the state of Georgia. Work began in 1927 on the face of Washington which was completed – appropriately – on 4 July 1930. Borglum died before the monument could be completed, but his son, Lincoln, finished the project in 1941. Each face measures 60ft from chin to forehead, twice the height of the Sphinx, and the largest individual donation toward the cost of the project was given by Charles E. Rushmore, the New York lawyer, after whom the mountain was named.

In her journal, Elizabeth Fry refers to a joint of meat as a **'mouse-buttock'**. What is, or was, it?

It conjures up some strange mental pictures but the boring truth is that any cut of meat that came to the table in a shape vaguely reminiscent of a mouse was known as a mouse-buttock.

Meat is muscle and the word muscle comes from the Latin *musculas* meaning 'little mouse'.

How many definitions are there for the word **mull**?

You asked for it!
To study or ponder as in 'mull over'.
To crumble or crush as in mill.
A promontory or headland, as in Mull of Kintyre.
The lips of a sheep.
The lowest of four qualities of Dutch madder.
A heifer or cow.
A snuffbox.
A thin variety of muslin.
A muddle or mess.
To dull or stupefy.
To make wine or beer into a hot drink.
To rub or anoint.
To fail at something. In the old days a cricketer might 'mull' a catch.
To give a granular surface to a plate.
An obsolete form of mule.
To work steadily without accomplishing much, (colloquial American usage circa 1880).

When does lamb become **mutton**?

In the trade, lamb is lamb for a year. Most lambs are born in the early part of the year and are sold as such until December. After that, although we may still buy the meat as 'lamb', it is known as hoggets. Beyond eighteen months the meat is called mutton, now a rarity in high-street butchers since most of it goes to ethnic butchers or for processing.

In racing circles they use the word '**nap**'. What does it mean?

The tipster's nap is his very best bet for the day. He or she may make several suggestions for likely winners, but only the best will be the nap. The term comes from the card game Napoleon, a form of whist where a winning hand is referred to as a 'nap' hand.

Where did the word **Nazi** come from?

It came from the name of the Party led by Adolf Hitler from 1921 until his death in 1945: the National Socialist German Worker's Party – NA-tional So-ZI-alistische Deutsche Arbeiter-Partei.

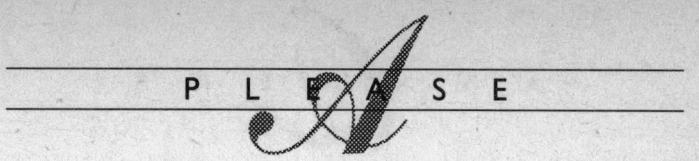

Did Nero fiddle while Rome burned?

How did they get **Nelson** to the top of his column in Trafalgar Square?

The famous monument to Lord Nelson was erected between 1839 and 1842 and is 170 feet (52 m) high. The statue itself, 17 feet (5.2 m) tall and designed by Edward Hodges Bailey, was put on view to the public before being hoisted into place. An estimated 100 000 people saw him at close quarters.

A web of scaffolding was built around the column and Nelson, weighing approximately 16 tons, was taken up in five pieces and assembled on the pedestal. However, a week before he was finally put in place, one of the oddest dinner parties ever was held on the top of the column where fourteen people sat down to enjoy a meal of rump steak!

It is a measure of the importance of the monument that Adolf Hitler planned to remove it to Berlin after he had conquered Britain as a symbol of his world domination.

Did **Nero** fiddle while Rome burned?

Certainly Rome burned but equally certainly Nero did not fiddle – the violin wasn't invented for a further 1500 years.

In AD 64, the tenth year of Nero's reign, there was a huge fire that destroyed much of Rome. He was an extremely unpopular Emperor, noted for his despotism and cruelty, and it was widely believed he had started the fire himself. Edward Gibbon, in *The History of the Decline and Fall of the Roman Empire*, says that Nero 'enjoying the calamity that he had occasioned, amused himself with singing to his lyre'.

How new is the New Forest?

It was new to William the Conqueror. He set aside the area as a royal hunting ground in 1079, drew up a set of regulations for the local people and named it Nova Foresta.

Did Isaac Newton really get hit on the head by an apple causing him to develop his theory of gravity?

The story as he told it is that while walking in an orchard he *saw* an apple fall and, looking up at the moon, wondered whether or not the force that caused the apple to fall might not stretch as far as the moon. If it did, that could be what held the moon in its orbit. But then again maybe it was just a story he made up!

What is the lowest denomination note ever printed in England?

The half-crown. A half-crown and a five-shilling note were both printed in 1941 but never went into circulation.

Is the nursery rhyme 'Ring a Ring o' Roses' connected with the Great Plague of 1665?

> Ring a ring o' roses,
> A pocket full of posies,
> A-tishoo, a-tishoo,
> We all fall down.

It is widely believed that the 'Ring a ring o' roses' referred to the sores associated with the plague, the posies were the herbs carried to ward off the infection and the sneeze confirmed you had failed to do so. But there is no evidence to support any plague connection and a great deal to suggest otherwise. Samuel Pepys wrote extensively about the plague and never mentioned it, nor does any of the many other accounts between then and our time. There are no records of the game itself being played until the 1880s and similar games occur across much of Europe and America. Furthermore there is no suggestion of any connection between the rhyme and the Great Plague before the Second World War.

Iona Opie, the leading authority on children's games, suggests the legend may have been started by an Oxford academic in the 1940s and spread like the plague itself!

Incidentally the custom of saying 'bless you' after somebody has sneezed is also said to be a relic of the plague – wrong! That practice is mentioned in *The Golden Legend* printed by Caxton in 1483.

For how long did an oak tree provide Charles II with a hiding place?

After his defeat at the Battle of Worcester in 1651, Charles II fled from the pursuing Roundhead soldiers and hid with his aide Colonel Carless in the branches of an oak tree at Boscobel in Shropshire. He stayed there from noon until dusk when he was taken to a hiding place under the floorboards in Boscobel House. Undignified it may have been for a monarch, but it enabled Charles II to flee to France and await

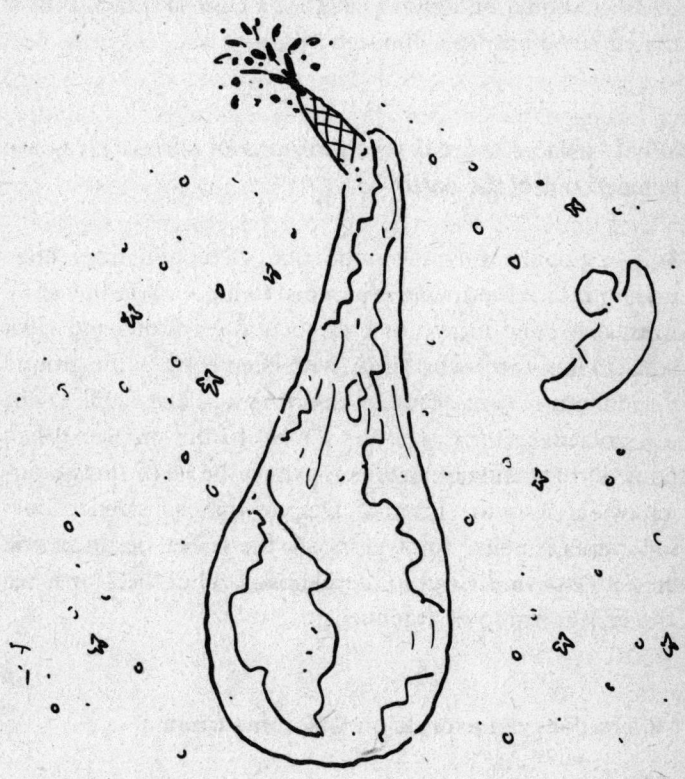

*What replaces the oil when millions of barrels a day
are pumped out of the earth?*

his return to the throne in 1660. He decreed that his birthday, 29 May, should be Royal Oak Day, a custom which is now remembered only in a pub sign.

What replaces the oil when millions of barrels a day are pumped out of the earth?

It is a popular misconception that oil comes from huge underground caverns and is pumped to the surface. In fact oil is usually found in porous rock such as sandstone and what replaces it is water which may have been lying in the ground for millions of years. Even in desert regions like Saudi Arabia it is ancient water that forces the oil to the surface. When none occurs naturally, engineers extract the oil by first pumping water into the ground. Despite this, subsidence does sometimes happen. Some years ago the seabed began to sink beneath one of the rigs in the Ekofisk field of the North Sea and its legs had to be extended.

Where does the expression OK come from?

This is one of the great unknowns. There are dozens of suggested derivations but consensus has it that it originated in America in the nineteenth century as a jocular abbreviation of 'oll korrect'. The first recorded use of OK was in Boston in 1839 and the following year President Martin van Buren adopted it as his election slogan. It was particularly appropriate for him because his birthplace in New York was Old Kinderhook, which was also his nickname.

Who was the Old Bill who gave his name to the Police Force?

There are many suggestions for the origin of the name. Here are a few of them:

William IV was on the throne when the Metropolitan Police Force was formed in 1829.

A 'Bill' is described in the dictionary as 'a weapon carried by Constables of the Watch until the late nineteenth century'.

It could have come from the song, 'Won't You Come Home Bill Bailey', 'Bailey' referring to the Old Bailey – the Central Criminal Court.

The original vehicle used by the Flying Squad had the index letters BYL.

The most likely suggestion however is that it comes from a popular First World War cartoon character, drawn by Bruce Bairnsfather, called 'Old Bill' – the Tommy who spoke for the troops in the trenches. 'Borrowed' by the government, who dressed him in the uniform of a Special Constable, he was used on posters to pass on good advice. His messages always began with the words 'Old Bill says . . .'

Why do onions make people cry when they peel them?

Onions don't want to be peeled. Like many plants that are bitter, or in some cases poisonous, onions use their smell as a defence mechanism. When the surface is cut it releases very fine droplets of a liquid which irritates the surface of the eye causing it to produce tears to wash it away. There are count-less ways of preventing onions from making you cry. Delia Smith swears she's tried them all and not one of them works!

We have William of Orange, Orangemen in Ulster and the Orange Free State. Any connection?

The family name Orange originated from a medieval principality in Provence and became the royal family of the Netherlands. England, looking for a Protestant king to replace the Catholic James II, invited William of Orange to rule with Mary in 1689 – which may have been a popular move in England but not in Ireland where Catholic support was strong. William went to Ireland and fought and won the Battle of the Boyne where his supporters (Protestants) were known as Orangemen. The Dutch soldier Robert Jacob Gordon in 1777 named a river in South Africa Orange River, in honour of a Prince of Orange (same family), and the river in turn gave its name to the state.

When was the Order of Merit instituted and why?

Edward VII introduced it in 1902 having been impressed by a similar honour in Germany. It is restricted to twenty-four members at any one time, including the sovereign. It also currently includes Sir Yehudi Menuhin.

Who was St Osyth?

Described as a 'virgin and martyr' she lived around 675 AD. She was the daughter of a Mercian chief and was brought up in a nunnery, possibly in Aylesbury, before being married off to the king of the East Saxons. However, on the wedding night just as her husband tried to consummate the marriage (against her will), a stag passed by and off went the king in pursuit. Osyth fled, went to live with a bishop, and established a monastery at Chich near Clacton which was sacked by pirates who cut off her head. Her body was taken to Aylesbury but was later returned to Chich where a priory was established in her name in the twelfth century. The village of St Osyth grew up around the priory and there is also a St Osyth Creek, St Osyth Marsh, St Osyth Well and St Osyth Wick.

P.S. Locally St Osyth is pronounced 'Toosey'.

Who invented the **parachute**?

Who knows? It evolved. There is speculation, but no proof, that the Chinese had such a device 2000 years ago. However what is certain is that Leonardo da Vinci drew designs for a parachute in the fifteenth century and the first successful descent (from a balloon) was made by Andre-Jacques Garnerin at Monceau Park, Paris, on 22 October 1797. The first man to parachute from an aircraft was Lieutenant Albert Barry at St Louis, Missouri, on 1 March 1912.

Spare a thought for a man named Edmund Maitland who pioneered the device in Britain. Even though he broke both ankles as a pilot in the First World War, he took to flying airships and parachuting. He always carried one in his luggage and whenever possible would disembark from the airship by parachute. In 1919 Maitland flew the Atlantic in the R34 but, on arrival in New York, found no ground staff waiting for him. He dispatched one of his crew, Lieutenant Pritchard, down by parachute to organize things. Pritchard was therefore the first person to arrive in America having flown the Atlantic and when asked by a journalist what he thought of the country he replied 'Hard'! Maitland and Pritchard were killed along with many others on board the airship ZR-2 in 1921.

Larry **Parks** was famous as the man who mimed to the voice of Al Jolson in the film *The Jolson Story*. Did he have a singing voice of his own?

Yes, Larry Parks was a singer in his own right who made several records in the days of 78s which have never been reissued. He and his wife Betty Garrett, a Hollywood actress, came to Britain in the early 1950s on a concert tour. Thousands turned out to see them and thousands were disappointed because Parks did not put on black make-up and did not sound like Al Jolson!

Which came first, the photograph or the **passport?**

The passport and by many years. Passports were originally 'safe conducts' personally signed by the monarch until the reign of Charles II. The earliest still in existence was issued on 15 June 1641 and is signed by Charles I. There were no photographs in passports until the outbreak of war in 1914. They became a standard requirement when adopted by the League of Nations Conference on Passports in 1920. Even with the new machine-readable European passport a photograph is still required.

St **Patrick** is credited with driving the snakes out of Ireland. Is it true there are no snakes there and, if so, why?

Legend has it that St Patrick banished the snakes from Ireland but the real reason is rather less dramatic. During the last Ice Age Ireland, like Britain, was covered in ice and the snake population was wiped out. When the thaw set in, the snakes returned to Britain from Europe across a land bridge where the Channel now is. However by the time they reached Wales the ice had melted and the sea level risen so there was no way for them to get across to Ireland.

Why is the **pelican** used as a Christian symbol?

The pelican has always been considered a particularly unselfish bird. It was thought to have the remarkable habit of pecking at its own chest and allowing its young to feed off its blood and this came to be seen as a powerful Christian symbol. Dante refers to Christ as '*Nostro Pelicano*' and other references can be found throughout medieval literature. Unfortunately the myth is just that – a myth. The bird does not engage in self-mutilation. It has been suggested that there may have been some confusion with the flamingo which secretes blood in its mouth and spits it out.

It is necessary to have different **pet food** for cats and dogs?

Dogs would fare pretty well if fed nothing but tinned cat food because dogs are omnivorous and can survive on a low-protein, or even meat-free, diet. Cats are true carnivores and need relatively high quantities of animal protein so would fare rather worse if fed only tinned dog food. If a cat could be persuaded to become vegetarian it would die.

Is there any truth in the story of the **Pied Piper** of Hamelin?

It is an old tale and well-known long before Robert Browning wrote his famous poem of that name in 1834. (Incidentally, Browning knew the story from his father who also wrote a poem about it.) The earliest reference is in 1450 when the historian Heinrich von Herford tells how, on 16 June 1284, a handsome young man appeared on the streets of Hamelin playing a silver pipe and led 130 of the town children out through the East Gate and away, never to be seen again. The story may have its origins in the Children's Crusade of 1212 when about 50 000 children set out from France and Germany to capture Jerusalem. It might also have come from a local feud in 1260 which resulted in the death of most of the young people of Hamelin. Nobody knows.

It is necessary to have different pet food for cats and dogs?

Who was the Pimm who invented the drink which bears his name?

We don't know much about James Pimm. He owned an oyster bar in the City of London and set up a chain of restaurants, the last of which were sold in the late 1960s. In 1841 he invented his famous Pimm's Cup recipes. Pimms No.1 is gin-based, No.2 whisky-based, No.3 brandy-based, No.4 rum-based, No.5 rye whisky-based and No.6 vodka-based. The gin-based and vodka-based Pimms are the only ones still made today. Only six of the top men in the firm knew the precise recipe and they still have to sign an undertaking never to reveal the secret.

When is Plough Monday and what used to happen on that day?

Plough Monday is the first Monday after Twelfth Night and it marks the end of the Christmas holiday. It was the day on which men were supposed to return to work – or to plough. In the farming community one of the customs was to pull a plough from door to door collecting money for a final binge. Another custom was to stage a play with standard characters such as St George and the Bold Basher.

Women were not so lucky. They were expected to return to work on the day after Twelfth Night regardless of the day of the week. Consequently 7 January became known as St Distaff's day because women returned to their distaffs (daily occupations) on that day.

Why are plus fours so called?

Plus fours are the baggy knickerbockers that flop down below the knees which are worn principally by golfers. They were made with an extra four inches of material hence 'plus four' and a more extreme style were known as plus eights.

Before you ask, knickerbockers were named after Dietrich Knickerbocker the fictitious author of Washington Irving's *History of New York*.

Why do polar bears not get frozen feet when they walk on ice?

Polar bears can withstand extreme cold because of their thick oily fur, thick skin and the layer of fat which covers their body. They also have layers of fur and thick skin on the bottom of their feet. Their large body mass helps to keep their blood warm as it circulates and they have only small extremities, such as their ears, to cool it down.

Why was Portsmouth known as Pompey?

As with so many interesting questions the answer is far from clear but here are a few suggestions:

The football club adopted the name before the town. The original team was made up of members of the Royal Artillery, known as the Pompeys because their opposite numbers in France had been recruited from the fire brigade or '*pompiers*'.

At the mutiny at Spithead in 1797 one of the main vessels involved was the Pompée.

In 1781 a group of British sailors from Portsmouth climbed Pompey's Pillar in Alexandria which earned them the name Pompey's Boys.

Portsmouth has traditionally been a great naval base and in Shakespeare's *Antony and Cleopatra* there is the line 'Pompey is strong at sea . . .'

Why are the British known as **Poms** in Australia?

The term probably came from the word pomegranate. The newly arrived British immigrants (also known by the nickname 'Jimmy Grant') were recognizable by their pink sunburned cheeks, and apart from Poms, in the early days, were often called 'Jimmys' or 'Jennys'.

When did the **pools** start?

The first football pool in Britain was started in 1922 by ex-Coldstream Guard officer John Jervis Barnard from a one-room office in Birmingham. The number of coupons returned in his first year was not even sufficient to cover his postage bill. The following year he was on the point of abandoning the scheme when, for a reason he could never explain, the coupons began to flood in and success was assured. Barnard sold out to David Cope in 1938 and the company became known as Cope's Pools. Littlewoods Pools started in 1923. The winning dividend paid out in their first week was £2.60!

Remembrance Sunday falls in November so why is the **poppy**, which flowers in May and June, the emblem of the First World War?

In 1915, *Punch* magazine printed a poem by John McCrae, a Canadian medical officer and soldier, called 'In Flanders' Fields' which spoke of the poppy as the symbol of death. It so moved Moyna Michael, an American whose house was being used by the YMCA for an international conference, that she bought 25 poppies, wore one and gave the remainder away to conference delegates. Madame Guerin, of the French YMCA, picked up the idea and started selling artificial poppies (made by injured servicemen and women) for charity. From that came the first official Poppy Day on 11 November 1921.

Initially all poppies were made in France but after the formation of the British Legion in 1921 Earl Haig established the first British poppy factory in Bermondsey. The factory has now moved to Richmond and is the sole supplier to the Poppy Appeal of 40 million poppies a year.

Do **porcupines** really shoot their quills at an attacker?

No. The quills of a porcupine are only loosely embedded in the animal's skin so that when they impale an attacker, quills are left behind. The myth has arisen because the quills are sometimes so loose that they are dislodged when the porcupine flicks its tail.

Why should you always pass the port to the left?

According to tradition it should always circle the dinner table clockwise. Unless you are the host, you should never pour the port for anybody else. The host may fill the glass of the lady on his right who would otherwise have to wait. In reality, this is the most sensible way to pass a heavy object around the table. Most people are right-handed – they take the port from their neighbour with that hand, pour a glass, and pass it on.

When did postcodes start and what do they mean?

The first postcode was introduced by Rowland Hill in 1856 when he divided London into four sections according to the points of the compass. Numbers were not added until 1917 and other big cities adopted the system at the same time. Postcodes for machine sorting were introduced on a trial basis in Norwich in 1959 and the present national system was introduced in 1974.

To take an example: CW5 5RB. CW5 (the 'outward code') denotes the area to be Crewe and the district, Nantwich. 5RB (the 'inward code') is for the sector and unit which sorts the mail down to just a few houses. There are 120 postcode areas, 2 900 districts, and approximately 9 000 sectors making up 1.7 million postcodes around the country.

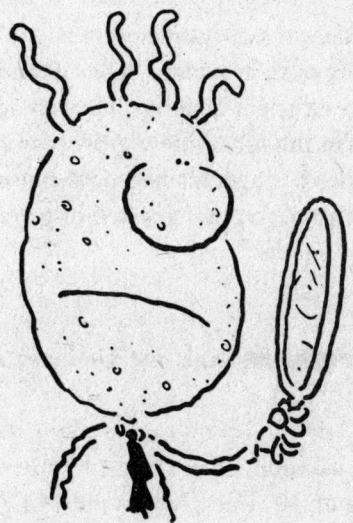

Why is it unwise to eat potatoes that have begun to sprout?

Why is it unwise to eat **potatoes** that have begun to sprout?

Potatoes contain toxic substances known as glycoaloids which form part of their natural defences and can be poisonous if eaten in sufficient quantity. They are found in greater concentrations in the tuber's new growth and also when the skin of the potato has been damaged or exposed to light. So it is always wise to cut out any bruised or green parts of potatoes and its new shoots.

How much **pressure** does the air exert on the human body?

At sea level, a 'column' of air one inch square and stretching out to the edge of the atmosphere weighs 14.7 lbs (6.7 kg). A column of air one foot square weighs nearly a ton and the air pressure on the average human body is about fifteen tons.

What was, or is, the **Primrose League**?

The Primrose League was founded in 1883, two years after the death of Benjamin Disraeli, First Earl of Beaconsfield, and in his memory.

A group of people wished to express continuing support for the policies with which the Conservative Party, under his leadership, had come to be identified. These included support for the monarchy, the Empire, the Church of England and the law coupled with a commitment to social reform, the freedom of the individual and the growth of Britain's influence in the world.

Today the Primrose League exists as a non-party-political discussion group boasting a membership of around a thousand.

Who was **Public Enemy No. 1**?

John Dillinger was so active as a bank robber and murderer in the 1930s that he was named Public Enemy No. 1 by Attorney General Homer Cummings. Strangely he was never on the FBI list of the 'ten most wanted men', even though boss J. Edgar Hoover called him 'cheap, boastful, selfish, tightfisted and pug-ugly'.

Dillinger was shot dead in 1934 by FBI agents outside the Biograph cinema in Chicago having just seen his favourite actress Myrna Loy in *Manhattan Melodrama*. Fatally wounded, he fell to the ground without even drawing his pistol.

What makes a steam locomotive **puff**?

The water is boiled under pressure and passes through the regulator (the steam engine's equivalent of the car's accelerator) and into the cylinder where it pushes the piston that drives the wheel. On the return stroke, the steam has done its job and is pushed out of the exhaust valve and up the chimney to emerge as a 'puff'.

The average steam locomotive has two cylinders, so for every revolution of the wheel you get two puffs.

Will there ever be a puncture-proof tyre?

There is one now – almost! The tyre is filled with a silicon foam which expands and re-inflates it if the outer surface is broken. That enables the car to be driven for a further twenty or thirty miles with very little effect on its handling. At the moment they are mainly used by rally drivers.

What does the 'Q' mean at the start of some cars' numberplates.

The first letter on the numberplate denotes the registration 'year' of the vehicle (it runs from 1 August one year to 31 July the next). If a vehicle is not new but has nevertheless to be issued with a number then it has a 'Q' plate. For example, if a car has been registered abroad and is then imported into Britain, after a year it has to be taxed and so needs a British number. To differentiate it from a new car, which would be given a number from the current list, it is issued with a Q number.

What happened to William Quantrill, known as the bloodiest man in American history?

He was a man around whom many myths have grown up but he does seem to have earned his title. He was the leader of Missouri's largest guerilla gang fighting on the Confederate side in the American Civil War. Among the men who rode under his black flag were some of America's most notorious outlaws – Jesse and Frank James and the Younger brothers, Bob, Cole and Jim.

In 1863 he led a raid on Lawrence, Kansas, which resulted in a blood bath. One hundred and fifty people were slaughtered, including every single member of two squads of federal troopers stationed in the town. He also murdered 17 prisoners after defeating a Union cavalry detachment at Baxter Springs.

At the end of the war, some say Quantrill was on a one-man mission to assassinate President Lincoln when he was shot and fatally wounded in Kentucky. Three weeks later Quantrill was dead but the myth-makers say he survived and at heart was a kindly soul who went to Texas to take up his original calling as a teacher.

What is **quantum** mechanics?

Quantum is Latin for 'amount'. Everything at the subatomic level comes in 'amounts': mass, energy, momentum, etc. 'Mechanics' is the old term for the science of motion. So quantum mechanics is the branch of science that investigates the behaviour of subatomic particles.

After the General Election, the **Queen** invites the leader of the winning party – the Prime Minister if the same party is returned to power – to form a government. What would happen if that person had just lost his or her seat?

Because we have no written constitution there is no set procedure for what would happen; nor is there a precedent to follow because it has not occurred in modern times. The nearest we came to it was in 1964 when Patrick Gordon-Walker lost his seat but was still made Foreign Secretary until a safe-seat by-election came up. Sadly for him he lost that too and had to resign. If a party leader lost his seat, the Queen would probably still ask him to form a government, provided the party wished him to continue as leader, and a safe seat would be found as soon as possible.

All this begs another question: how can a non-elected person sit in the Commons and run the country? He can't! But the Cabinet is not part of the Commons, although obviously it is answerable to it.

Does the **Queen** need a passport to travel abroad?

The Queen does not have a passport – she could hardly issue one to herself! – but all other members of the royal family require passports and visas in the normal way. The Queen is however subject to customs formalities, both in the UK and other countries, which conjures up some intriguing mental pictures!

Why does the **Queen's** head on our coins look to the right while her father, George VI, looked to the left?

This is not political bias in the monarchy but tradition. Ever since the seventeenth century and Charles II, the direction the monarch's head faces has switched each time the throne has a new occupant. Why? One suggestion is that it was Charles II's way of turning his back on Oliver Cromwell who had beheaded his father.

Who are the **Queen's messengers**?

They are usually retired service personnel who spend a great deal of time on aircraft with one eye on the luggage! Their duty is to escort diplomatic bags containing sensitive material which, under the Vienna Convention, can be carried through international frontiers without examination.

The emblem of the corps is a silver leaping greyhound which has been in use since the time of Charles II.

Boxing is governed by the **Queensberry Rules**. Who was he, and when were they drawn up?

The Marquis of Queensberry has two claims to fame. In 1895 he was accused of libelling Oscar Wilde who he believed was having a homosexual affair with his son, Lord Alfred Douglas. The Marquis won the case and Wilde was ruined socially and financially.

It was the same Marquis of Queensberry who in 1860, with John Chambers, founded the Amateur Athletics Club to encourage boxing contests. He was a great patron of the sport which had fallen into disrepute with the rise of prize-fighting. In 1867 Chambers, under the supervision of the Marquis, drew up the rules of the sport which included making the boxer wear gloves and fight over a series of three-minute rounds. Ever since they have been known as the Queensberry Rules.

Why is a **quid** the slang name for a pound?

In the eighteenth century, when pickpocketing was a thriving business, people would carry the occasional gold coin in their mouth, about the only place a pickpocket couldn't reach. The other thing frequently in the mouth was a plug or 'quid' of tobacco. Hence 'put your money where your mouth is'. Strange but probably true!

What was the **Quinby** flying machine?

Watson F. Quinby was an American and his is only one of many patents taken out for flying machines. In 1872 he described in great detail how the intrepid aviator strapped on a huge pair of wings, attached to a harness with a pair of stirrups, and then . . .

> 'It is intended to start from the ground. In order to make a beginning one foot is disengaged from the stirrup when – by raising the other foot and pushing the hands upward and forward as in swimming – the wings are raised. Then, by suddenly depressing the wings, by means of an elevated leg, the former are intended to elevate the body by this action on the air. This alternate elevation and depression of the wings is continued as long as flight is desired. After rising from the ground the other foot may be inserted in its stirrup and both legs used. The actions are intended to be natural resembling those of swimming in water.'

In 1911 the US Patent Office started to ask for working models of some of the more unlikely inventions!

Who invented the Qwerty typewriter keyboard layout?

The first practical typewriter was invented by Christopher Scholes and Carlos Glidden in Milwaukee in 1867 and was marketed by Remmington in 1874. Scholes, who was a printer, designed the layout of the keys to minimize the chance of jamming when a typist is typing at speed. There have been a number of attempts to rationalize his design, but none so far has been successful.

Until the 1950s you travelled either 1st or 3rd class on the railway. What happened to 2nd class?

There used to be three classes but it was soon found that people either wanted to travel as cheaply as possible (3rd class) or in extra comfort (1st class). The demand for 2nd class was very small and by 1870 most railway companies had abolished it. However, because there were three classes on French trains, the service to and from the Channel ports continued to offer all three classes until 1956.

How does Britain's rainfall compare to that of other countries?

Britain's wettest place is said to be Styhead Tarn in Cumbria with an average annual rainfall of 172.9 inches (over 14 feet). However the world's wettest place is Tutunendo in Colombia where the annual rainfall averages 463.4 inches (over thirty-eight feet), so we could be a lot worse off! We do have our moments though: two inches of rain fell in twelve minutes in 1970 at Wisbech in Cambridgeshire and tales are told of the afternoon of 31 May 1682 when nearly two feet of rain fell in 'a quarter of an hour'.

What is the **Rathbone Society** and when was it set up?

The Rathbone Society exists to help people with learning difficulties achieve their full potential. It was founded in 1920 by Elfreda Rathbone whose cousin, Lillian Greig, had adopted a child labelled 'mentally defective' and excluded from school. Lillian Greig proved that, given the right training and support, such a child could develop and progress. She opened a kindergarten for similar children in 1916 and Elfreda Rathbone was one of her teachers. Sadly Lillian Greig and the child died in a flu epidemic, but Elfreda Rathbone was determined that the work should continue and so the society that bears her name was formed. Today they have twenty centres throughout the UK offering a range of services to people with learning difficulties.

When were 45 rpm discs introduced in Britain and when was the last 78 rpm **record** released?

45s began to be introduced in 1953 by the two main record companies of the time, Decca and HMV. But there continued to be a market for 78s for several years among collectors and abroad. The last official 78 release was 1961 but there was a

How is rice grown and harvested?

further limited edition issued in 1970. The last 78s listed in the catalogue were a ten-volume set of the 'History of Recorded Music' and a few Royal recordings.

He's 'living the life of **Reilly**'. Who was Reilly?

He was probably a character in a Vaudeville song of the 1880s written by Pat Rooney which tells how he will:

> 'Swim in wine
> When the White House and capital are mine.'

He turns up again ten years later in another song by Charles Lawlor and James Blake called 'The Best In The House Is None Too Good For Old Reilly'.

How is **rice** grown and harvested?

The seed is usually planted and grown in nursery fields for about three weeks before being transplanted into the flooded paddy-fields, although there are varieties of upland rice that do not require this watery treatment. It takes approximately three months to grow to maturity, by which time the crop can be about one metre high with the rice hanging in clusters at the end of the side shoots similar to wheat. At this stage it is known as 'paddy'. The fields are drained, the crop is harvested and then milled to remove the husk.

Rice that has had only the inedible husk removed is brown rice — otherwise it goes on to be polished white. So-called 'wild' rice is not rice at all but the seeds of a North American aquatic grass.

Is **rice paper** made from rice?

No. Bombay ducks are not ducks, catgut is not feline intestine and rice paper is not rice. Who knows how it came to be so called? Probably because it came originally from China and was different from the ordinary paper we know. Also it is used on the bottom of macaroons, is edible and might be assumed to be made from rice. In truth the Chinese made it from the soft pithy wood found in the centre of the trunk of a small tree called *Aralia Papyrifera* that grows in Taiwan. When it is not stuck to the bottom of macaroons it is used for making artificial flowers.

Why is the word **Roger** used when radio messages are being passed?

It is the equivalent of saying the letter 'R' for 'message Received and understood' in the old phonetic alphabet (Alfa, Bravo, Charlie etc). Nowadays, in the international alphabet 'R' is Romeo – but good old Roger remains.

The **Romans** landed in Britain in 55 BC. What date would that have been to the Romans?

The Romans measured their years from the date of the foundation of Rome in 753 BC. So to them the landing in Britain would have occurred in 698.

The **Romans** were master builders and engineers but how did they manage without a system of mathematics such as our own?

It is true the Romans could not do sums as we do. They had no zero and there were no calculations between numbers like 5 (V), 50 (L) and 500 (D), although complex calculations could be done using an abacus. However, most of their engineering skills were developed by trial and error and building was governed by well-tried rules of proportion and design. Most calculations could have been done in their heads and measurements could then be written down using their symbols.

The gypsy language is **Romany**. Where did it, and they, come from?

The gypsies have always been a nomadic and rather mysterious people. At one time they were thought to have come from Egypt – hence the name 'gypsy'. They and their language originated in Northern India and spread from there in a series of migrations. In the eleventh century they were in Persia, by the fifteenth century they had arrived in Western Europe and today they are spread around the world.

The Romany language reflects their wanderings and is similar to other languages of Northern India but with the inclusion of words borrowed from the countries in which they stayed. It is an oral language, with no written tradition, which is part of its strength. Romany can only be learnt by living close to gypsies and has become almost a secret language which bonds the people together and by which they recognize each other.

In chess which came first, the name rook or castle?

The piece may look like a castle but in the early Moslem and Indian game it was a chariot – *ratha* in Sanskrit. When the game was introduced into Europe, *ratha* was corrupted into the Italian *rocco*, meaning tower. In time, *rocco* became rook and the piece was made to look like its new name.

Why is the Rose of Jericho also known as the Resurrection plant?

The Rose of Jericho is a plant native to Western Asia which has the remarkable ability apparently to rise from the dead, hence it is sometimes called the Resurrection plant. During the dry season the leaves drop off and the branches curl inwards until it becomes a dry lifeless ball which is blown about by the wind. However when it finds water it expands again, leaves grow and it produces a tiny white flower.

What is rosewood? Are there rose trees large enough to produce timber?

Rosewood is so called because it has a sweet rose-like scent and is used for making fine furniture. It comes from various trees of the genus *Dalbergia* found in Brazil, Honduras, Jamaica, Africa and India. Honduran and Brazilian rosewoods are generally considered the best.

What is the Royal Institute for International Affairs and what is its function?

Both the Royal Institute for International Affairs and its American counterpart were set up after discussions between British and American delegates to the Paris Peace Conference in 1919. They are self-governing, owing allegiance to no political party, and are funded by grants from various sources. George V granted the Institute its Royal Charter in 1926 and confirmed its function as that of providing and maintaining 'a means of information upon international questions'. In other words, if you want to know something about international politics try them for an answer. They are based at Chatham House in London.

What is royal jelly and does it do you any good?

Royal jelly is a thick white mixture of proteins, carbohydrates, minerals and vitamins that is secreted by worker bees and fed to their larvae. Those that receive this preferential treatment throughout their development become queens while the remainder add to the army of humble workers. Because it appears to have this remarkable quality it has long been thought to have miraculous rejuvenating abilities. However, despite extensive scientific research there is no evidence to suggest that it can make people look younger or live longer.

We have a Royal Society for the Protection of Birds but only a National Society for the Prevention of Cruelty to Children. Why?

Do not be misled by the title. It does not mean that the royal family has more regard for the protection of birds than children. Both societies operate under Royal Charter – in the case of the NSPCC, since 1895. The Queen and the Queen Mother are patrons of the NSPCC and Princess Margaret, who is the working president, has even appeared on *The Archers* to talk about the society's work.

To qualify for a 'Royal' title, an organization has to apply to the Home Secretary, who advises the Queen and the NSPCC has never applied. They claim 99% of the population know them by their initials and it would be foolish to change. Besides which they like to stress they are 'national', looking after the interests of children throughout the British Isles.

When dismissed from a job why is it called getting the sack?

One colourful suggestion comes from Turkey where sultans who had tired of their wives were known to have had them sewn up in a sack and thrown into the Bosporus. Such 'sackings' were also said to have taken place in ancient Rome when wives who failed to please ended up in the Tiber. However the less dramatic, but probably more correct, explanation comes from medieval times when workmen carried the tools of their trade around with them in a sack which would be left at their place of work. When his services were no longer required he would be told to go – and handed his sack.

The scarab beetle is a dung beetle. Why was it worshipped by the ancient Egyptians?

The scarab was seen as a symbol of creation and resurrection. They believed there were only males of the species and that they self-created out of the ball of dung they constantly carried around. What we know, and the ancient Egyptians did not, is that the beetle lays its eggs in the dung ball and carries it around both as a protective measure and as a food source when its larvae hatch.

Who was Schneider whose trophy was competed for in air races during the 1930s?

Jacques Schneider was the son of a wealthy French armaments manufacturer and the French Under-Secretary for air. He was born in Paris in 1879 and had the good fortune to witness the first flight of the Wright brothers in 1903 after which he was hooked on flying. In 1912, to help France maintain her lead in aviation, he instituted an air race for seaplanes and put up the trophy and £1000 prize himself. It was won for the first time in 1913 by Marcel Prévost with a speed of 45.75 mph.

The trophy changed hands several times before it was won

outright by Britain after victories in 1927, 1929 and 1931, the last with a world record speed of 340.08 mph.

Jacques Schneider died in 1928 but his trophy can now be seen in the Science Museum in London alongside the winning plane – the famous Supermarine S6B designed by R. J. Mitchell – the forerunner of the even more famous Spitfire.

In the Crimean War, how did the hospital at Scutari come to be equipped with a drying machine provided by Charles Dickens?

Dickens, who always had a strong social conscience, funded a hospital for women who had fallen on hard times which had one of these machines installed. He first heard about them from the governor of a London prison. They measured about 6 feet square by 7 feet high and from all reports they were extremely efficient, capable of drying all the items inside in twenty-five minutes.

Florence Nightingale heard of the machine through one of Dickens' co-funders, Angela Burdett-Coutts, and decided such a thing would be invaluable for her hospital in Scutari. So Dickens had another one made and shipped out to the Crimea where Florence Nightingale said it was 'invaluable'.

Is it true that seaweed was used to soundproof Broadcasting House?

Not quite. An issue of the *Architectural Review* of 1932, dedicated to the building of the new Broadcasting House, reveals that the wall cavities are filled with eelgrass, which is an aquatic plant although not seaweed. The Dorchester Hotel in London's Park Lane, built around the same time, is also insulated with the plant.

What is selenium? It is contained in some vitamin pills and yet it is possible to die of selenium poisoning.

Selenium is one of the so-called trace elements essential to a healthy diet. It is from the same chemical family as sulphur and is found in soil. We obtain our normal supply naturally through fruit, vegetables and cereals. Curiously the people of China suffer from a selenium deficiency because it is lacking in its soil. However in other than minute quantities selenium and its compounds are extremely toxic – hence selenium poisoning.

How did the self-heating soup, issued as emergency rations to soldiers during the Second World War, work?

In the bottom of the tin was a separate sealed compartment that contained, in effect, a firework mixture! Pulling the ring-pull was the same as lighting the blue touchpaper. The chemical mixture ignited and, after a few moments, the can could be opened to pour out the hot soup. It came in two flavours, oxtail and mulligatawny, and was made by Heinz.

They stopped producing it around 1970 because hygiene regulations no longer allowed the 'firework' chemicals to be used in a food factory. However similar products are still available today.

Why is the opening shot in tennis called the service?

It goes back to the days of real tennis, played at Court by the aristocracy, which was at the height of its popularity in the sixteenth century. It was considered undignified for a royal person to start a point so, at the call of 'Service!', a servant would appear with ball and racquet to start the play. He would then withdraw and leave the court to the noble protagonists before stepping forward to start the next point.

What is the difference between a shire and a county?

In practice there is no difference. In Saxon times the shire was an administrative area presided over by a 'shire-reeve' or sheriff. After the Norman Conquest the shire began to be replaced by the French word *conté* – originally land in France owned by a count. *Conté* became county and eventually became the accepted word.

Is sirloin so called because King Charles II dubbed it a knight?

Charles II was dining on some excellent beef and is quoted as saying 'For its merit it should be knighted and henceforth called Sir Loin.' Dr Johnson refers to the story in his dictionary as 'a title given to a loin of beef which one of our kings knighted in a fit of good humour'. That however is the end of the story, not the beginning. The name was already in existence in the French *sur longe* – above the loin. So the King was making a gracious pun.

Why do we talk about the **$64 000 question**?

There was a radio quiz in the 1940s in America called *Take it or Leave it* in which the prize doubled every time the contestant answered a question correctly – it later came to England as *Double Your Money*. The prize started at one dollar and doubled up to two, four, eight, sixteen and thirty-two, with a final question worth sixty-four dollars. The game then moved to television where it was played not for single dollars, but thousands. So the ultimate question, the one that could solve all your problems (?), was the $64 000 question.

Is one hour's **sleep** before midnight worth two after?

There is nothing magical about the midnight hour, but there is some sense in the old saying. We sleep in cycles of approximately ninety minutes duration, alternating between deep sleep and 'dreaming' sleep – known as Rapid Eye Movement sleep. As the pattern starts with deep sleep, we sleep more heavily when we first drop off than later in the night.

What animal has the keenest sense of **smell**?

It's difficult to be certain of the answer to such a question, but the male silkworm moth must take some beating. To announce her presence for mating the female releases a substance called bombykol which the male can detect even when diluted to one molecule in a quadrillion (10^{15}) of air. This

must make bombykol the ultimate perfume! Or could it be the male emperor moth which, according to experiments in Germany in 1961, can 'smell' a female at a range of 11 km.

How did an Englishman, James Smithson, who never went to America, come to found America's famous Smithsonian Institute?

James Smithson was the illegitimate son of Hugh Smithson Percy, 1st Duke of Northumberland, and Elizabeth Keate Macie. He was a brilliant scientist and knew most of the leading scientists in Europe and when he died childless in 1829, his considerable fortune was inherited by his nephew Henry Hungerford. Hungerford too died childless so under the terms of the original will the whole estate went 'To the United States of America to found at Washington, under the name of the Smithsonian Institute, an establishment for the increase and diffusion of knowledge'.

But why leave the money to America? The answer probably lies in his lingering resentment over the circumstances of his birth. He once wrote 'My name shall live in the memory of man when the titles of the Northumberlands and the Percys are extinct and forgotten'.

He may never have gone to America alive but in death he did. His remains were removed there in 1904 and are now interred in the original Smithsonian building.

What is the maximum number of points that can be scored in the game of **snooker**?

The usual answer is 147 – the maximum break made up of all fifteen reds each followed by a black and then all the colours. But if there are any points on the board (if a player has committed a foul shot) then his opponent could pot a colour in place of a red followed by a black, which would be an additional eight points. He would then have to clear the table for a total of 155. However there is no record of it having happened in an official competition.

Who discovered **soap**?

Legend has it that the discovery was made in Roman times by women washing clothes in the Tiber. They were made especially clean because the water contained a mix of melted fat and ash that came from the animal sacrifices regularly performed on mount Sapo – hence 'soap' (some say!). The Babylonians, 2800 years ago, boiled fats with acids to produce a soap-like substance, but whether they used it for washing or as a dressing for their hair is unknown. There are also biblical references showing that the Israelites mixed ashes and oil to produce another soap-like substance.

The modern industry began in 1690 in Boston when Benjamin Franklin started to sell soap and candles using a mix of fats and alkalis.

Why should the suburb of Southgate be to the North of London?

It was a gate not to London but to the south of Enfield Chase, a forest which once stretched across much of what is now North London. At its south gate was a hamlet called Southgate.

Is it true that by royal decree Cavalier King Charles spaniels have certain privileges denied other dogs because of their royal patronage?

Contrary to popular belief they are not the only dog allowed into theatres and they are certainly not allowed to ride free on public transport. It is known that Charles II loved the breed and on one occasion took one on board a yacht where it bit one of His Majesty's loyal servants in a particularly painful place. The victim was alleged to have said 'God bless your Majesty, but God damn your dog'!

There is a grain of truth in one of the myths about the rights of the breed – they are said to be the one dog allowed to run off the lead in the Royal parks. This was true in the past but by convention rather than decree, royal or otherwise.

What is the origin of Speakers' Corner in London's Hyde Park and are there any restrictions on what people are allowed to say?

Speakers' Corner came about after protests over the second Reform Bill drawn up by Disraeli in 1866. There were riots in many parts of London, the most notorious being the 'Battle of the Railings'. This was a pitched battle between the police and demonstrators in Hyde Park when railings were torn up and used as weapons. To attempt to disperse further violence, the Police Chief agreed to allow the protesters to have their uninterrupted say in the corner of the Park by Marble Arch and so in 1872 Speakers' Corner came into being.

There are no legal rights protecting the Hyde Park orator, merely an understanding with the police. They insist there must be no blasphemy, obscenity or incitement to violence. Nor can speakers claim immunity from the laws of the land such as slander. If you would like to have your say, the place to do it is Speakers' Corner on Sundays and Tower Hill on weekdays.

The earth is revolving on its axis and we are revolving with it. At what speed are we travelling and why is there no sensation of movement?

If you were standing on the equator you would be travelling at 1000 mph. In Britain we are moving at about 500 mph. If you were standing at the North or South Pole you would not be travelling at all – you would be spinning on the spot!

Do spiders have ears?

We have no sensation of movement because everything, including our atmosphere, is travelling with us at the same speed. In addition to that movement, the earth is rushing around the sun, the sun is travelling around the galaxy and the galaxy around the universe.

Do **spiders** have ears?

Not as such. They do however, have sensitive hairs on their bodies that can detect movement and changes in air pressure. So although they cannot hear the names you call them they may take fright and run away.

Is **spondulicks** meaning money a real word?

It is an American slang word coined in the nineteenth century by American humourists in imitation of the vogue among serious writers for using Latin and Greek words. Mark Twain used it in *The Adventures of Huckleberry Finn*: 'I'm darned if I'd live two miles out of town – not for all the spondulicks.' It was also a favourite word of the late W.C. Fields.

What is **St Elmo's fire**?

St Elmo's fire is a luminous flickering phenomenon, usually seen around tall objects such as church spires and ships' masts, caused by atmospheric electricity. The discharge is not strong enough to be dangerous but superstitious sailors took it as a portent of bad weather.

St Elmo is a corruption of St Erasmus who, legend has it, was rescued from drowning by a group of Neapolitan fishermen and in gratitude he promised to display a warning light on board ships at the approach of a storm. Not surprisingly, St Elmo became the patron saint of sailors.

Who made the **Stalingrad sword** and why?

It was made by Wilkinson Sword Ltd of Acton and was presented to the people of Stalingrad by King George VI.

An eighty-four-year-old blacksmith was said to have been brought out of retirement to forge the sword which has an inscription in Russian on one side of the blade and English on the other: 'To the steel-hearted citizens of Stalingrad, the gift of George VI in token of the homage of the British people'. It was to commemorate the heroic defence of Stalingrad against the German army during the Second World War and was presented by Churchill in Tehran in 1943. Stalingrad is no more – it has been renamed Volgograd – but the sword can still be seen in the museum there.

How are used **stamps** able to buy a guide dog?

Charities such as Guide Dogs for the Blind sell the stamps in bulk to dealers who, in turn, sell them on to collectors, mainly abroad, in mixed bags. Dealers are interested because among the thousands they occasionally find a real collector's item.

What is the difference between **statute** law and common law?

Laws which are made by Parliament and pass on to the statute book are statute laws. Those laws are then enforced by the courts and the way in which judges interpret them in individual cases leads to common law, built up by precedent. Incidentally, the term 'common-law wife' has no meaning in English law. A woman cannot obtain the legal status of a wife without going through the marriage ceremony.

What British **summer** was the driest and hottest on record?

The hottest summer was 1976 when the average mean temperature for the three months June, July and August was 17.8°C (64°F). Temperatures of more than 32°C (89°F) were recorded on 13 consecutive days from 25 June to 7 July.

The driest summer was 1800 when only 74 mm (2.9 in) of rain fell in the three summer months. In 1976 there was 76 mm (3 in) of rain.

What happened to the **sun** during the ice age?

Nothing – it was still there. The tilt of the earth's axis in relation to the sun leads to seasonal changes. The side of the earth leaning toward the sun will enjoy its summer while the side leaning furthest away will be experiencing winter. The tilt is 23.5 degrees but scientists have calculated that during the ice age the tilt became more extreme. This led to exceptionally cold winters and to summers which were not warm enough to melt the ice which had formed.

However the tilt of the earth varies on a 42 000-year cycle. The earth also wobbles on a 23 000-year cycle. To add to the confusion the earth's orbit is neither circular nor constant but varies on a 100 000-year cycle.

Scientists also estimate that there have been about twenty ice ages so far and predict another one just around the corner.

What is the origin of the word **taxicab**?

The cabriolet was a small two-wheeled horse-drawn carriage with a folding hood which gave way to the Hansom cab. The taximeter was fitted to them at the end of the nineteenth century to record the fare automatically based on the length of the journey. When motorized cabs were introduced in 1907 the name taxi or taxicab stuck.

How did the scoring system in **tennis** come about?

The rules for lawn tennis were formally drawn up for the first Wimbledon Championship in 1877 and were based on the system used in real tennis. In the French version of the game the scoring was done on a clock face at the side of the court. As points were won, the hands were moved through a quarter – hence 15, 30, and originally 45. Somewhere along the way 45 became 40, but nobody seems to know why.

'Deuce' derives from the French *deux* (a player must be two points ahead to win the game).

'Love' comes from *l'oeuf*, an egg signifying a nought. And you 'set' the number of games to be played.

We know what the **Third World** is, but what are worlds One and Two?

The French demographer Alfred Sauvy claims to have coined the expression Third World in 1952 to describe the countries that do not have sophisticated industrialized economies. Using the French Revolution as an analogy, where they had the three 'estates' – the clergy, the aristocracy and the people – he wrote, 'Like the third estate, the third world is nothing and wants to be something'. The expression was later used at an Afro-Asian conference in Indonesia in 1955 and became the title of French magazine, *Le Tiers Monde*, in 1959.

How was **time** broadcast and how were clocks set before we had the wireless?

The home of time was Greenwich Observatory and before 1852 you either had to go there to set your chronometer or you had to watch for the 'time ball' – a red ball which was hoisted on the mast on the Observatory roof and dropped on the stroke of one o'clock. The spread of the railways made the distribution of accurate time a necessity so, in 1852, the 'Shepherd's Master Clock System' began. A master clock in Greenwich sent out a signal through the telegraph network

Did the band play on on the Titanic?

to 'slave' clocks at stations and post offices up and down the country. On the hour, telegraph operators flicked a switch and all messages had to wait, literally, while 'time' passed!

Did the band play on on the **Titanic**?

The *Titanic* had been declared unsinkable so there was no immediate sense of panic when the ship hit an iceberg near Newfoundland on her maiden voyage in April 1912. The impact, which tore a hole in the hull below the water line, was hardly felt and there were even reports of people playing snowballs on deck. Lifeboats had been provided for only about half the number of people on board. Even so, the first ones left only about half full – so convinced were the passengers that the *Titanic* could not sink.

When the truth dawned, there was a scramble for seats in the remaining boats while those passengers left behind resigned themselves to the inevitable. The millionaire Guggenheim, who had given up his seat for a woman, instructed his valet to lay out his evening dress so he could die like a gentleman. And the ship's band 'played on' – a mixture of hymns and cheerful dance music. Two and a half hours after the collision, the *Titanic* sank beneath the waves.

What does the word **tog** mean on a duvet?

The 'tog-rating' is a measurement of the thermal insulation of the duvet. The higher the figure, the more warmth the duvet will retain. The value is arrived at by putting the duvet over a heat source and measuring the heat loss over a given period of time. The word comes from the slang for clothes – togs.

The American system is slightly different. They have the CLO-scale which compares the insulation ability against the standard US army uniform.

How did the town of **Tombstone** in Arizona get its name?

When a prospector named Ed Schieffelin told people he was looking for silver in the foothills of the Dragoon Mountains he was told, 'The only thing you'll find in those hills is your tombstone'. So when he found a rich vein of ore and staked his claim, Tombstone was the obvious name for the place.

What is the origin of the **topping-out** ceremony?

The completion of a building is still marked by the topping-out ceremony to ward off evil spirits and bring good luck. It is a custom which goes back to pre-Roman times. The two essential elements are that a fir tree should be fixed on the highest point of the building and that there should be beer for the workers. Custom decrees that if beer is not provided the workforce will fly a black flag and the building will never prosper.

Topping-out is often taken as seriously as the laying of the foundation stone and many a pin-striped Chairman of the Board has found himself climbing on to the roof of his building for the first, and probably the only, time.

Why are track events in athletics always run anti-clockwise?

Because that is how the ancient Greeks ran their races. Athletes in the stadium would run the 'stade', go round a post at the far end and back to the start, and the tradition has continued. Anti-clockwise is also the direction approved by the International Federation of Amateur Athletics, but there are exceptions. In the last century, both Oxford and Cambridge Universities had tracks which were run clockwise – Cambridge's still is but Oxford changed over in 1948.

There is also said to be a medical reason for preferring to run anti-clockwise. Some believe that because the heart is on the left side – the inside of the track – running that way is easier. But there is no scientific evidence to support this theory.

When were the first traffic lights installed?

A Mr J. P. Knight, a railway signalling engineer, devised the first set of 'traffic lights' which were installed in Bridge Street outside the Houses of Parliament in London on 10 December 1868. There were two lights, red and green, which were gas-powered and changed by hand. Sadly in January 1869 they blew up killing a policeman operating them and they were abandoned in 1872.

We had to wait for the arrival of the car for them to be tried again. In Cleveland, Ohio, they introduced a two-light system in 1914 and the first three-light system appeared in New York in 1918. Britain's first set was placed at the junction of Piccadilly and St James's in London in 1925.

We serve soup in a tureen. What is the origin of the word?

The Vicomte de Turenne is one of France's great historical military figures becoming Marshal General in 1660. The story goes that on an occasion when there were no bowls in which to serve the soup, the Vicomte gallantly whipped off his helmet and used that instead. We ought to add that there are tedious people who suggest the word may have derived from terrine, an earthenware dish.

Why are royalty given a twenty-one-gun salute rather than, say, twenty or twenty-two?

It all dates back to 1689 when it was decreed that guns should be fired 'to salute persons of quality going into or coming out of any of Their Majestys' castles, forts or blockhouses', and on special occasions such as the King's birthday. The number of shots was not specified and probably depended on the number of cannon available. By 1829 it was felt that the situation was chaotic, with different number of rounds being fired for different people on different days. So what was the answer? Set up a committee! In 1831 it began its deliberations and in 1836 it finally concluded that a 'Royal Salute shall consist of twenty-one guns at all saluting stations' – except those at St James's Park and the Tower of London where it was to be forty-one. And that's how it remains today, except that in 1923 the saluting station at St James's Park was moved to its current home at Hyde Park.

Why do stars or distant lights **twinkle**?

The twinkle of a star is caused by variations in the air temperature. The same effect is often produced when looking at an object at the end of a sunbaked stretch of road. The heat from the road surface causes the air close to it to rise up through the colder air above. This produces turbulence and the light waves passing through are refracted slightly leading to distortion. So it is our own atmosphere that prevents us from seeing the stars clearly – hence the need for the Hubble space telescope.

What causes the body to **twitch** occasionally as we fall asleep, causing us to wake up with a start?

Not only are these twitches quite normal and fairly common, they also have a name: myclonic jerks. They are caused by a 'neurological discharge' – in other words a discharge of some of the body's electricity down the nerves causing the muscles to twitch.

*What causes the body to twitch occasionally as we fall
asleep, causing us to wake up with a start?*

What do the initials UHT on milk mean?

It stands for Ultra Heat Tested. The milk, orange juice or even soup is heated to a very high temperature to kill off bacteria and then packed under sterile conditions. The contents will keep for several months. However once opened and exposed to the air it behaves like any other fresh product and will keep for only a few days in a fridge.

When did Britain acquire the habit of carrying umbrellas?

As the name suggests (Latin – *umbra* – shade), umbrellas were first used to keep off the sun and almost 4000 years ago the Egyptians considered them a status symbol. It is thought the Greeks introduced them into Europe, but it was the Romans who first used them as a protection from the rain. After the fall of Rome they disappeared only to return to Britain in the eighteenth century. A man named Jonas Hanway became very unpopular with London's coachmen who feared that if his strange contraption, called an umbrella, was to catch on they would be out of a job. (Nowadays it is quite the opposite. The moment the umbrellas go up the cabs disappear!)

Who was **Uncle Sam** who gave his name to the United States?

He is thought to have been a man called Samuel Wilson – an honest, hard working, self-made man who was an army supply inspector in the war of 1812. There was an actual incident recorded by an eyewitness when goods from a merchant named Elbert Anderson had been marked E.A.U.S. (for United States). 'Here's one for Uncle Sam!' said one of Sam's workmen and the term stuck. It first appeared in print in the *Troy Post* (an upstate New York daily newspaper) on 7 September 1813.

Who said **Uncle Tom's Cabin** started the American Civil War?

Abe Lincoln himself said it. Harriet Beecher Stowe, urged on by religious zeal and members of her family, decided to write about slavery. The result was *Uncle Tom's Cabin: or Life among the Lowly* which came out first in serial form in a religious magazine and was an instant success. The first print run of the book in 1852 sold out in two days and by the end of the year sales had reached 300 000 copies. Ten years later, when the Civil War was at its height, Harriet Beecher Stowe met Abraham Lincoln who said, 'So this is the little lady who made this big war.'

Was London's Underground system steam-driven when it was first built?

Yes. It was opened in 1863 with the Circle and Metropolitan lines which were steam-driven. But as the tunnels were much closer to the surface than most of the system today, ventilation was not the problem you might imagine. Electrification came in 1890 when the first deep level section was opened between Stockwell and King William Street, and within fifteen years most of the system had been electrified. There was, however, one section officially part of the Underground between Amersham and Rickmansworth (which runs on the surface) that was not electrified until 1960!

Which is correct, Union Jack or Union Flag?

This is one of the common mistakes that irritates the experts. Correctly it is the Union Flag or Banner. But since all flags flown from a jack-staff are called 'jacks', Union Jack can be correct.

What is the longest speech ever made at the United Nations?

Fidel Castro of Cuba, never a man to use one word when two will do, addressed the General Assembly of the United Nations on 26 September 1960 for four hours twenty-nine minutes.

Is it really necessary to **unplug** the television at night. Is it not sufficient to switch it off?

The British Safety Council recommends the plug be taken out of the socket as a safety precaution, even if there is a switch, for two reasons. Firstly, switches are notoriously unreliable, particularly if the house has not been rewired recently. Secondly, because TV sets work on very high voltages the condensers retain power for a long time. If you completely unplug, this gives the set time to dissipate the power overnight. If left plugged in but switched off, the power does not dissipate so easily. So there is the possibility of a surge of electricity going through the set when it is switched back on which could blow the tube.

Who gave us the idea of **Utopia**?

Thomas More (later Sir Thomas), one time Chancellor of England, put forward his idea for the perfect state in 1516 in his book, *Utopia*. Taken from the Greek meaning 'nowhere', it described an imaginary island representing the perfect society. Nineteen years later he was to realize he lived in a far from utopian state when he was beheaded for refusing to accept Henry VIII as head of the church.

Who invented the **vacuum** cleaner?

Hubert Booth in 1902. His first machine was a horse-drawn affair that was parked in the street with a length of hose to suck out the dirt indoors. It became extremely fashionable and housewives were constantly asking for demonstrations. Booth even developed a transparent hose so that the dirt could be seen being sucked up. Known as the 'Noisy Serpent', it proved unpopular with cab drivers who regularly sued Booth because, they claimed, it caused their horses to bolt.

Who was St **Valentine**?

He was a Christian saint and martyr who died in Rome in AD 269 and he has nothing to do with the custom of sending cards on 14 February. In pagan Rome the fertility festival of Lupercalia, when girls would put their name into a 'love urn' and boys played lucky dip, was celebrated on 15 February. Rather than make themselves unpopular by attempting to abolish such a popular festival, the early Christian Church transferred it to the feast day of St Valentine, who thereafter became the patron saint of lovers.

Who invented **Vaseline**?

Vaseline is the trade name for the petroleum jelly, petrolatum. When the British chemist Robert Chesebrough was working in the oilfields of Pennsylvania, he noted that the men used the residue that built up around the pumps to soothe cuts and burns. He tested it on himself and developed a purified commercial version which came on to the market in 1878.

Chesebrough claimed to eat a spoonful of his wonderful discovery every day thereafter. He lived to be 96!

Do we have a recording of the voice of Queen **Victoria**?

In the Royal Archive at Windsor Castle is a letter from Sydney Morse, a solicitor (no relation to Samuel of Morse code fame), asking the Queen if she would allow him to record her voice. She agreed and in August 1888 at Balmoral she recorded a few words into a graphophone machine. That recording, along with several others, is said to be in the Science Museum in London. But despite the use of modern technology the sounds are unintelligible – all that can be said is that there is a woman's voice on the cylinder.

The Royal Archive also tells us that in 1889 Queen Victoria recorded a message – thought to be a regal greeting – for the Emperor of Abyssinia. It was sent with instructions for it to be destroyed after use – and as far as we know it was.

Why do they roll out the red carpet for VIPs?

Red or purple has always been the colour of the gods, partly because it symbolized blood and suffering and partly because it was a difficult, and therefore expensive, dye. Red carpets were reserved for priests and ordinary mortals were not allowed to step on them, a rule broken by Agamemnon when he returned victorious from the Trojan wars. He had a red carpet unrolled for him only to be murdered by his wife for his troubles. But red is not the only colour of ceremony. The sacred colour of the Chinese emperors was yellow.

Who were the virgins who gave their name to the Virgin Islands?

St Ursula is said to have made a pilgrimage from Cologne to Rome accompanied by 10 999 other virgins. On their return they were massacred by Attila the Hun. Christopher Columbus, on his second voyage in 1493, remembered the legend when sailing among the dozens of small islands in the West Indies and thus called some of them the Virgin Islands.

Why are volcanos cone shaped?

When magma, the molten material that comes from the earth's interior, is spewed out from a single fissure, the cone is formed from the ash that falls back on top of it as it solidifies.

Do any members of the royal family have to vote?

The only members disqualified from voting because they are in the royal family are the reigning monarch and the Prince of Wales. Apart from those who are peers, who are also disqualified, all others are as eligible as the rest of us. In practice, none of the royal family close to the throne exercise their right to vote – Lord Linley is the only royal known to have case his vote in recent elections.

Is it true that the Great Wall of China can be seen from the moon?

We don't know because nobody has looked! Although claimed to be the only man-made structure visible from the moon, the truth is that the Apollo astronauts saw it when they were on their way back from the moon. So we know it can been seen from space, as was a hole in the Canadian forest (a result of tree felling) as well as pollution from industrial plants and the wakes of ships.

Who, or what, was 'Waltzing Matilda'?

Matilda wasn't a 'she', it was a rucksack; and she wasn't waltzing, she was bouncing from side to side when slung over the shoulder of a jolly swagman (vagrant worker).

Did the Battle of **Waterloo** make the fortune of the Rothschild family?

There is a story that the official semaphore signal of victory was cut off by fog after the words 'Wellington defeated'. The London Stock Market was unaware that the sentence finished '... Napoleon at Waterloo', and prices tumbled. This was greatly to the advantage of the Rothschild family who had heard the news some hours earlier by carrier pigeon.

Nathan Rothschild was very conscious of the value of news and operated his own courier system. He had agents in Dover, Calais, Ostend, Ghent and Brussels and postboys shuffled backwards and forwards across the Channel in fast boats. He had heard the news of Wellington's victory forty hours ahead of the official dispatch to Downing Street and tried to tell Lord Castlereagh, only to be informed that the Prime Minister was sleeping and could not be disturbed. Nathan Rothschild did purchase a large quantity of British bonds, but they only added to his already considerable fortune.

Which is correct, **Welsh Rabbit** or Welsh Rarebit?

It is a racist dish! Thanks to the English of the eighteenth century (and probably earlier) being superior at the expense of the Welsh. 'Welsh Rabbit' is the correct name – the suggestion being that they were so poor they could not afford meat and ate simple cheese on toast instead. There is an English rhyme:

Jenny Ap-Rice Hur Could Eat Nothing Nice
A Dainty Welsh – Rabbit? – Go Toast Her A Slice
Of Cheese If You Please, Which Better Agrees
With The Tooth Of Poor Taffy Than Physic And Fees.
A Pound Jenny Got And Brought To His Cot
A Prime Double-Gloucester All Hot, Piping Hot
Which Being A Bunny Without Any Bones
Was Custard And Mustard To Taffy-Ap Jones.

In America there is even a Welsh Rabbit fan club. Called 'The Welsh Rabbit Association' they make it their business to tell people it is 'Rabbit' and not the affectation 'Rarebit'.

Was Hollywood the first to say 'Don't fire until you see the **whites** of their eyes'?

No, but they have said it many times since. It comes from an incident at the Battle of Bunker Hill, fought in the American War of Independence, in 1775. Either US General Israel Pitman, General Joseph Warren or even possibly Colonel William Prescott, when faced with the advancing British, gave the order 'Don't one of you fire until you see the whites of their eyes.' Was it good advice? The Americans were defeated at the Battle of Bunker Hill but it helped to raise support for the revolutionary cause.

In the winter we hear a lot about the **wind-chill** factor. How is it measured?

It was the Canadian Air Force who began to evaluate wind-chill. It is a method of measuring the increase of heat loss with an increase in wind speed – in other words we feel colder on a cold day if the wind is blowing. The London Weather Centre uses what they call the Steadman Formula after the man who developed it. For example, a temperature of 0°C at five knots will measure −1.7°C whereas at thirty knots it dips to −13.3°C.

What are the names of the different sized **wine bottles**?

Magnum – two bottles
Jeroboam – four bottles
Rehoboam – six bottles
Methuselah – eight bottles
Salmanazar (Shalmaneser) – twelve bottles
Balthazar (Belshazzar) – sixteen bottles
Nebuchadnezzar – twenty bottles

Why most of them should be named after biblical characters is, according to one Champagne maker, 'unknowable, and one of the world's great mysteries'!

How much did the early **wireless** licence cost?

The earliest wireless licence was issued in November 1922 to people who wished to listen to the broadcasts of the British Broadcasting Company and cost ten shillings (50p). Later that same year a further licence was introduced to people who built their own sets, which also cost ten shillings. Demand was brisk, particularly for the latter, which upset the BBC because at that time it was a private company set up by manufacturers who would rather people bought their sets than built their own. So in 1923 the cost of the constructors' licence was raised to fifteen shillings (75p).

Why do we 'touch **wood**'?

One explanation of the old saying is that by touching wood you are invoking the safety of the cross, or the refuge of the sanctuary which was traditionally given to a hunted person who touched the wood of a church door. But the superstition goes back to pagan times when our ancestors worshipped the spirits of trees. Different trees were believed to harbour different spirits, the oak being perhaps the most important because it was home of the 'sky and thunder' god. To touch the tree meant to invoke the spirit of that tree.

What was the **world ice** theory?

It was a theory proposed by a mining engineer, Hans Hörbiger, who suggested that all planets are covered by thick layers of ice. The moon, he said, had a coating 140 miles thick.

According to the theory, this ice fell to earth as hailstones and large chunks of it caused sunspots millions of miles across. Hörbiger had his fans in the Third Reich – including Hitler, who was always an easy touch for a crank theory. He also believed that we on the earth lived on the inner surface of a huge sphere. Experiments were even done to photograph the British Fleet, located further 'up' the slope, by pointing infra-red cameras at an angle of 45° up in the air.

Do worms have a head and a tail? And can they re-grow when cut in half with a spade?

The earthworm does have a head and a tail. The head, or prostomium, is where the mouth and most of the sensory equipment is located and when cut in half (accidentally!) that portion is capable either of existing on its own or continuing to grow. There have been instances when the tail has regenerated and grown a new head, but that is very rare.

Does a worm feel pain when it is cut in half? Worms have five large nerve fibres that run the length of their bodies. They also have a simple brain, so it would be aware a cut had occurred. Whether or not it is correct to call that pain is a very difficult thing to say.

Who or what is the Writer to the signet?

They are the oldest body of lawyers in Scotland and their duties correspond to those of solicitors in England. They used to be the people who prepared writs to be passed to the sovereign for signing and sealing with his signet.

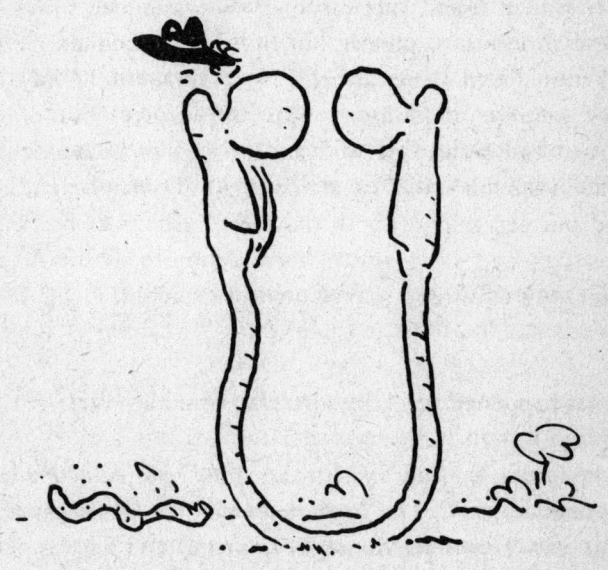

*Do worms have a head and a tail? And can they re-grow
when cut in half with a spade?*

Who was Douglas 'Wrong Way' Corrigan?

He was an Irish-American pilot who intended to fly from New York to Los Angeles, but ended up in Dublin. He took off from Floyd Benet airfield, New York, on 17 July 1938 and, because his compass was 180° degrees out of true, turned east instead of west and arrived in Baldonnel near Dublin the following day after a flight of twenty-eight hours and thirteen minutes with only forty gallons of fuel left. It was suggested it was always his intention to fly the Atlantic, but Douglas 'Wrong Way' Corrigan denied it.

What happened to Hitler's **yacht** after the war?

The Grille, as Hitler's yacht was named, was launched on 15 December 1934. The longest journey he made on it was from east Prussia to Memel in Lithuania and he was sick all the way. Hitler hated water. 'On land I am a brave man but at sea I am a coward', he said. And there is no record of him having set foot on the boat during the war years. The Grille was taken over by the Royal Navy in 1945 and sold as a merchant ship but was scrapped in 1951 at Bodens Town, New Jersey.

What is the origin of the word **yankee**?

It could have derived from the Yanko Indian tribe, whose name means invincible. Or from the Cherokee word *eankke*, meaning coward or slave and used by the Virginians to insult the New Englanders who refused to fight the Cherokee.

The most likely derivation comes from the Dutch word *janke* meaning John. Again it was also used as a derogatory term for the New Englanders but in time it was applied to North Americans in general.

Did the poet W. B. **Yeats** imagine his Isle of Innisfree or does it really exist?

It certainly exists. It is an island in Loch Gill in County Sligo about 120 miles north-west of Dublin. It was a childhood memory for the poet which he wrote about when living in Holland Park in London. Sadly, when he went back to the area, he was unable to find it again because it was only one of several islands in the lake.

Why do birds seem particularly fond of eating the heads of **yellow** primula?

Birds have an acute sense of colour. Why would they often be so highly coloured if they were colour blind? They probably see more colour in the spectrum than humans – hummingbirds for example can detect ultraviolet.

But do they have a preference for yellow? In the case of some birds it seems so. Sparrows in spring can make short work of a bed of yellow crocuses, but unfortunately nobody so far has come up with a satisfactory reason why.

What are the **yellow** symbols – diamonds, circles and squares – seen on many major road signs?

They are there in case of major accidents or emergencies when heavy traffic may have to be routed in particular directions. At such times, drivers will be told to follow the 'yellow-circle route' or the 'yellow-square route'. The Department of Transport does not want them used on a regular basis as 'rat runs' for motorists to escape traffic jams, so many of the signs on major roads are covered up and uncovered when needed.

Is **Yma Sumac** a Peruvian pin-up or was she really plain Amy Camus?

Yma Sumac was one of the pop phenomena of the early 1950s with her incredible four-and-a-half-octave voice and exotic looks. But there were those who said she was a housewife called Amy Camus who had simply reversed the spelling of her name. Most however, including *Time* magazine, believed her story that she was born in 1922 in Ichocan in the Peruvian Andes and was descended from the Inca Kings. Her full name was Zoila Imperatriz Chavarri Sumac Del Castillo. She went to America in 1947 and was a gift to the image-makers with her voluptuous figure and strange costumes. Her songs were said to be based on Inca chants and Yma was still giving concerts in 1987. Perhaps only Yma Sumac and the CIA, who were interested in her during the 1950s, know the full story.

'I haven't seen him for **yonks**!' Derivation please?

Who knows, but there is a general consensus that it is an army expression which started in Cyprus in the 1950s. It could be the result of telescoping 'donkeys' years' or one ingenious suggestion says it is shortened from Y-ears, m-ONths and wee-KS. Surely too clever by half!

How did the **Yucatan** peninsular get its name?

The Yucatan is the spit of land that juts out from Central America towards Cuba. It was the centre of Mayan civilization and when the Spanish *conquistadors* arrived in the sixteenth century and asked what the area was called, they got the reply, 'Yucatan', which in fact simply means 'what do you want?

Nietzsche wrote *Thus Spake Zarathustra*. Who was **Zarathustra**?

Zarathustra, or Zoroaster, was a preacher in ancient Persia around 1200 BC. The religion named after him, Zoroastrianism, was, like Christianity, known as a salvation religion. Life is a struggle between good and evil: the good is embodied in Ahura Mazda (the creator) and the evil in Angra Mainyu (the hostile spirit). Man has the freedom to choose between the two. It was the official religion of the Persian Empire.

What is a **ziggurat**?

They were temples erected by the people of Mesopotamia, usually a series of rectangular boxes built on top of each other and diminishing in size, they often had a shrine on top. The tower of Babel was probably a Babylonian ziggurat, built to make a 'celebrated name' for the builders. The tallest to survive is the one found in Ur, now in Iraq, although only the first and part of the second storeys remain. The largest on record was built by King Untash around 1250 BC. Known as the 'Ziggurat of Choga Zanbil' it had five tiers and was about fifty metres (164 feet) high.

What is **zircon** – known as the 'poor man's diamond'?

Zirconium silicate, to give it its proper name, is a mineral of variable colour. Usually brown, it can also be grey, green, blue, yellow or even colourless. Some translucent varieties are cut into gems. Zirconium, its principle element, has a high melting point, is extremely resistant to corrosion and is used as a coating for fuel elements in nuclear reactors.

The oldest 'rock' known on earth is a grain of zircon estimated to be 3.96 billion years old.

Contributors

Hadrian Jeffs, D J Parsons, Craig Hamilton, Mark Douglas, Mike Bingley, Kate Marsh, David Rigby, Edward Grace, Julie Geoghean, Melvin Cook, Alan Hobden, Arthur Stonebrook, Angela Mullings, R A Laundon, Madelayne Rogers, M G Shirley, Doris Miazek, Ken Hamilton, H A Jackman, Duncan McVee, P Lowey, R C White, O Chorthon, Veronica Deacon, Gerry Osborne, George Hirst, J Weeden, Anthony Lewin, Charles Hammond, Helen Bullock, Mrs Eleanor Horwood, Peter Carter, Peter Burton-Wilkins, Lorely Edwards, Frank Cregan, Valerie Heudebrourck, Gillian Escott, Margaret Cawley, Brian Young, Douglas Bowen, G Gough, Dorothy Leech, Betty Kay, Maureen French, F Pover, Deidre Owen, Bob Burke, Mary Macdiarmid, Clare Norman, F J Hayward, Margaret Ellis, Mrs Deacon, Diane Butler, Leslie Henshilwood, Elizabeth Craddock, R S Atkins, Jim Higgins, Alan Hunt, D G Scott, Colin Ambler, Mrs A L Inglis, F W Bailey, Hugh McKeown, E J Hamlin, Mrs A Randall, Ann Cosker, Jackie Tilson, J F Pedley, Jennifer Curtis, Jenny, B Dach, Eva Catch, Mrs Dorothy Hughes, Robert Butler, Geoff Wootten, A McCarthy, Geoffrey Gardner, Graham McLean, D Stephenson, John Newton, R Softley, Eric Russell, Mrs P Tidy, Bill Baxter, Jim Western, W Edwards, J P Marren, Jack Cooper, Michael Whittaker, Georgina Watham, Rick Jordan, John Richardson, Michael Press, Robert Vincent, Margaret Morley, Albert Phillipson, Doug Hamilton, M J Howe, Jane Maxwell, Ingrid Derbyshire, Sophie Wallace, Gill Drake, Derek Turner, E J Sharp,

J Kelly, Eileen Dean, Miss Joyce Page, E F Smyth, Margaret Cutts, Mrs Gill Forrest, M Stewart, Alan Taylor, J M King, T Franklin, Derek Lowe, Bob Hellier, Rosa Giovanna Hago, Maureen Lucas, Tony Boyle, Michael Wetherby, J Simmons, Katherine Oads, John MacRae, Peter Kitching, Jane and Kate Ferguson, R Green, Mrs H Robinson, Chris Anderson, S H Furlunger, Jacqui Dando, Eliza Hammet, Emily Goldsmith, Alan R Hunt, Jamie Campbell, Carol Hancox, A Myerscough, Jill Targett, Carol Cooper, Elaine Morris, Barry Dutton, Christina MacLeod, W Wood, M Hall, Terry Sercen, Chris Devereux, Jackie Dawes, Patrick Preston, Mrs Corinne Allen, Richard Ashton, Alaine Talby, H W Coburn, George Sumpter, Helen Burbage, Ann Walker, Ted, W G Snell, Richard Sergant-Manse, Rob Fleming, Joan Gardner, Alan Maplass, D Harris, Mrs M L Lammas, Victor Trill, P Bartlett, Jerry Brown, Sid Barber, Anthony Philips, Leslie Plews, Elizabeth Wheeler, Ray Halsall, Mrs Peggy Greenman, H Cliffe, Sam Morley, Bernard Fairclough, D Brown, Mrs M Jane Ensor, Stanley Murison, Derek Stewart, Jim Thornton, Abigail Mauzer, Evelyn Pearce, Alan Nash, Mary Ann Dunbar, Bill Turnbull, Ian Beattie, Jack Mott, Harry Faires, John Shannon, Barry Baxter, John Poppleton, Gerald Smith, Jenny Brennan, Kathleen Littlefair, Audrey Pidsley, Roy Pett, M J Lalley, Jill Baker, Norma Rowe, Mrs Jan N Rushe, T K Morris, Jack Temple, L C Stopp, Madeline McCarthy, Nora Clark, Denis Perry, Sheila White, W Wood, Pat McClarnon, Sarah Ann Brown, Joan Williams, Glenis Barron, G R Hartley, L G Ralphs, Jane Ponder, Jim Bowes, Joanne Philpott, Chrissie Walker, Miss Hull, Fred Easterbrook, Clive Whicker, Bran Forrester, H S Crosher, John Hacombe, Mr & Mrs Topham, Mrs P Simmonds, Bill Campbell, Miss J D Catt, Rose Croft, Doug Fothergill, Katherine Burgess, Mrs P Helen, S Spiers, Rita Tapp, Hazel

Jones, Cliff Lake, Margaret MacDougal, Kevin Munday, Valerie Nareike, Brian Fearnley, Edna Trumble, Tony Murray, Mrs E Kemp, John Brooks, A Anderson, L Jackson, Ralph Goodridge, Michael Rhodes, Mrs Joan James, Dr W H Cartwright, Mrs Louise Darley, Frank Macklin, James King, Jacqueline Warren, Richard Nobbs, Alan Dickson, David Elliot, Bob Shaw, Charles Orville, Doreen Barnes, A Shenton, Mrs Jilly Gordon, Steve Mason, E Ferdz, Veronica Booth, Mrs A S Hawes, Miss Penny Lord, Mike Ninnim, David Cox, Grace Dix, David Bailey, Albert Phillipson, Bert Brightwell, Ray and Lucien Groutage, Mrs Eileen Lloyd, Kay High, Jim Roberts, H W Bailey, James Mallott, Margaret Kelly, Rob Davis, Mrs S Waldridge, John Marchington, Mrs Heather Findlow, Bob Hellier, Graham Cross, I Rosser, Martin Ives, Mrs A Wiggin, Mrs Catherine Morgan, Simon Caley, Joel Carter, Emrys Williams, Jack Penzer, Jim Pocock, John Ford, Hannah Pinkerton, Joan Moth, Margaret Cutts, Graham Todd, Miss G Field, Mrs Jean Hunter, Dennis Bingham, Miss Ann Beal, R Croden, Mr J E D Headon, Harry Ebbs, P Burton.